An Incomplete Guide to Qualitative Research Methods for Counsellors

Pete Sanders
and
Damian Liptrot

PCCS BOOKS
Manchester

First Published in 1994
PCCS BOOKS
Paragon House
48 Seymour Grove
Old Trafford
Manchester
M16 0LN

© PCCS BOOKS
All rights reserved.
No part of this publication may be
reproduced, stored in a retrieval system,
transmitted or utilized in any form by
any means, electronic, mechanical,
photocopying or recording or otherwise
without permission in writing from the
publishers

An Incomplete Guide to Qualitative Research Methods for Counsellors

ISBN 1 898059 04 7   0046616

Cover design by Peter Kneebone
Printed by Printoff Graphic Arts Ltd. Alexander House,
Lomeshaye Road, Nelson, Lancashire.

Contents

Introduction		i
Chapter 1	**Understanding a Qualitative Approach**	1
	The role of the researcher	3
	Variables and measurement	4
	Treatment of data	5
	Purpose of research	7
	Qualitative work and counselling	8
	Compare and Contrast # 1 14	
Chapter 2	**Approaching Qualitative Research**	17
	Some important questions	17
	Women's perspectives - feminist research	20
	Ethnocentricity in research	24
	Ways of organising your research	24
	All studies are...	25
	Surveying the data	27
	Case studies	28
	Evaluation studies	31
	Compare and Contrast # 2 17	
	Compare and Contrast # 3 26	
Chapter 3	**Preparing for Qualitative Research**	35
	Calibrating your instrument	35
	Literature review	36
	Your cover story - uncovered	38
	Gaining access	40
	Location of research	41
	Choosing people to work with	43
	Rapport	43
	Trustworthiness	44
	Your pilot study	48
	Your research proposal	50
	Practical considerations	54
	Ethical considerations	57
	Compare and Contrast# 4 45	

Chapter 4	**Qualitative Data Collection**	63
	What is data?	64
	Chapter 4 overview	67
	I Observing others and ourselves	68
	II Interrogating others and exploring their experience	88
	III Looking at what's left behind	108
	IV Other methods	111
	Compare and Contrast # 5 107	
Chapter 5	**Treating Qualitative Data**	117
	Some useful questions	117
	Methods of data treatment	122
	Coding	122
	Describing	124
	Categorising	125
	Sorting	127
	Typologies	127
	Using time: chronologies	128
	Content analysis	130
	Discourse analysis	136
	Repetition of research cycle	136
	Participant consultation	137
	Compare and Contrast # 6 121	
	Compare and Contrast # 7 134	
Chapter 6	**Presenting Qualitative Research**	139
	Reporting your work	139
	The process of writing your report	142
	Formal reports	142
	Reports required by others	146
	Communicating to a wider audience	147
	Compare and Contrast # 8 140	
References		149
Recommended further reading		151
Glossary		153
Index		157

Introduction

This book is the final part in our tour of research and associated activities for counsellors. It is quite different form the first two, as it should be, since they deal with quantitative research methods and the statistical analysis of quantitative data. The present book is an attempt to cover as much of the ground as possible with definitions and explanations along the way. It is an introduction to qualitative research for the uninitiated. We have tried to give a flavour of qualitative work, but readers will have to go to the recommended reading to get a real sense of what qualitative research is in real life. To encourage readers to explore the literature, the examples used in this book are taken where possible from well-known studies or work that has entertained us over the months of writing. This means that the examples are not all from the world of counselling, but we believe that they can be easily adapted.

In order to avoid the book simply becoming a running debate concerning the differences between qualitative and quantitative methods, we decided to 'box off' the discussion into *Compare and Contrast* panels. You will find eight scattered throughout the book.

As we came to proofread the book, we found that it was initially easy to mis-read a 'quantitative' this and 'qualitative' that, and to get the two terms hopelessly muddled in our minds. We tried various devices to ease the confusion and finally had a couple of bold italicised letters put in the middle of each word to help distinguish them more clearly; qua*l*itative and qua*nt*itative, respectively.

We did this in Chapter 1 only, thinking that the effect would irritate after a while, and hoping that by the end of Chapter 1 the confusion will have cleared for most readers.

Any unreferenced examples are entirely fictitious, being invented by us with tongue firmly in cheek, as we hope is clear in the text.

Finally, and most importantly, we gratefully acknowledge the following:
Firstly, The Association for the Teaching of Psychology for permission to use material from their pamphlet 'Ethics in Psychological Research' by Graham Davies, Goeff Howarth, and Sue Hirschler.
Secondly, our friends and family who have given us the encouragement and support we needed to see this project through.

Pete Sanders and Damian Liptrot
Manchester and Wigan 1994

1 Understanding A Qualitative Approach

As the late Bill Shankly once said, 'Football isn't a matter of life or death...it's more important than that'. Newcomers to the world of social sciences research would be forgiven for thinking they had stumbled into an ideological war zone when people start debating the pros and cons of qua*n*titative versus qua*l*itative research methods. When people write 'We must recognize the implicit violence of the standard academic approach' (Reason and Rowan 1981 p.487) we counsellors, trained as we are in spotting the subtleties in human communication, will realise that feelings are indeed running high.

This introductory chapter tries to explain the battle lines, although in fairness it has to be said that in recent years there has been a good deal of bridge building to find some ground on which both parties can stand safely without coming to blows. When we are first introduced to social science research, it is often in terms of 'scientific' methods, numbers and statistics. If your first reaction to this is terror, then on introduction to qua*l*itative methods you may feel lost in vagueness and confusion. So what is the debate all about? What is qua*l*itative research?

At the heart of the issue lies a *fundamental* difference in philosophy. This difference is not a new one and should be familiar to counsellors since a variation of it appears in the philosophies underpinning different counselling approaches. This difference is fundamental because it is in many ways irreconcilable and exclusive. In other words it is difficult, if not impossible, to hold both views at once, rather like religious views. You either believe in God or you don't. It is difficult to build a world view on a 'maybe' or a 'yes and no' answer. Such views are also often held with some passion and many people are not open to changing these views. It's not that people are rigid when it comes to thinking about social science research, it's just that rather like finding a counselling approach that is congruent with their personality, people discover that certain approaches to research resonate with or are more in accord with their views on life, the universe and everything.

This fundamental philosophical difference can be expressed in many different ways; it is the difference between:

• structure	structurelessness or chaos •
• outcome	process •
• objective	subjective •
• external frame of reference	internal frame of reference •
• neutral and detached	involved •
• 'science'-centred	person-centred •
• analysis	synthesis •
• taking apart	putting together •
• variables are identified and measured	complex variables that interact and are difficult to measure •
• numbers	thoughts, feelings, words, patterns •
• reduction to simple units	welcomes complexity and pluralism •
• people as objects	people as persons •
• measurable and observable	experiential •
• abstraction of facts	description of experiences •
• deduced from fact	intuition •
• technology	nature •
• quantity	quality •

The overwhelming conventional wisdom of our technological culture is that we all process the world in rational and 'scientific' ways. Forming little hypotheses about the world, testing them and then acting upon our findings. It must surely follow then, that the way to find the 'truth' is to pursue the same 'method' in research. We put these words in quotes because each one carries with it assumptions and behind each assumption lies a debate. The main assumption is that there is no other way of looking at the problem. This way of looking at the discovery of 'truth' is called positivism and was the dominant research method, so much so that it remained more-or-less unchallenged for decades.

That we can even have this debate is a tribute to the pioneers of qua*l*itative research methods. The language used in research is at the heart of the debate for the same reasons that it lies at the heart of issues of oppression because of colour, gender, etc. Language is important because it interacts with our thoughts and feelings - helping define and give shape to them at the same time as being defined by them.

If we look in a little more detail at the meanings behind some of the words and phrases used in research (many of which appear on page 2), we will get a better picture of the positive features of a qua*l*itative position.

The role of the researcher
Both approaches recognise the powerful effect that the researcher has on the research, from choice of area to be studied, the hypothesis or question asked, through to the collection and treatment of data. Human beings have profound effects on other human beings, so our research method must acknowledge this and deal with this in some way. If the researcher gets too close to the subjects under study, s/he may influence their behaviour.

In qua*nt*itative studies, this recognition is expressed as an attempt to remove all trace of the researcher and the effects of their person from the research; to remove the contamination of the human touch. Elaborate controls are enacted to prevent the researcher from having any noticeable effect (see Sanders and Liptrot 1993, pp.104-107). Also, the researcher, being human, is likely to have *their* judgement adversely affected by too close proximity to the subjects under study.

In qua*l*itative studies, this human interaction is deliberately exploited. The researcher tries to understand the complexities of the effect they might have by getting involved in the study, possibly as a participant. Qua*l*itative methods seek understanding of the process of the effect of the researcher by empathic understanding rather than neutral objectivity.

> *The questions to consider are:*
> • *Which is the best position from which to understand the effect of the researcher? Outside or to one side of the 'action' - or right in the middle of it?*
> • *In order to collect the best data, should the researcher be involved in the middle of the process or neutral and detached from it?*

Variables and measurement

Measurement of something isn't quite as simple as it sounds. Even the most hard-line qua*nt*itative researchers will agree that accurate measurement of anything is impossible, it's just a question of what degree of inaccuracy you're prepared to put up with. Another problem is that very few things stay constant for long enough to make a measurement useful; as soon as you've measured it it's changed, so you have to measure it again, then it changes again, and so it goes on. Add to that the fact that when you measure something you nearly always change it; that is to say that the very act of measuring something causes it to change and thus invalidate the first measure.

All qua*nt*itative approaches are dependent upon measurement and can be seen as the constant (if, in some people's view, vain) attempt to measure things as accurately as possible, given all of the drawbacks. Variables are seen as elements of the world which the researcher controls and manipulates.

A qua*l*itative approach, on the other hand, takes either the view, 'If measurement is so problematic, why bother?' or the view, 'Measurement is an insult to, or violation of, the human processes we are seeking to sensitively understand.' and so proceeds to try to find better ways to capture the meaning in the world that has relevance to the study in hand. This search for better ways involves assuming that there is no such thing as 'objective' reality, but that reality is socially constructed. The best way of understanding reality, then is from the point of view of the main protagonists in the study.

Variables, then, are understood as elements of the world which emerge through a non-invasive process of inquiry and are then described or portrayed in the process of data collection. They are not seen as simple unitary items but as complex interwoven strands of experience the essence of which will be destroyed by inappropriate unravelling. *Description* rather than measurement is seen as the prime method of data capture.

The question to consider is:
- *Will measurement of the variables capture the meaning without distorting it or is measurement so intrusive and 'insulting' that it changes or even destroys the meaning?*

Treatment of data
Once you have captured the meaning of the world in some form of data, the question is, how are you going to make sense of it? It could be that the form in which the data comes - numbers, words, pictures, tape-recordings, etc. begins to suggest certain ways of treating it. On the other hand, it could be that we are so conditioned to count numbers that we just can't think of anything else to do with them! All kinds of research are to some extent the story of how much we are prepared to wrestle with ourselves and our preconceived ideas as we try to make sense of the data.

Untreated data as it arrives from collection is called *raw data*. It is usually a jumble of notes, numbers, lists, tapes, in an apparently undisciplined pile. We have likened this raw data in qua*nt*itative studies to a raw diamond (Sanders and Liptrot 1993 p.35). An apparently charmless stone within which lies beauty waiting to be revealed by the skill of the diamond cutter. Statistical description and analysis (Liptrot and Sanders 1994) are the 'diamond cutter's' tools.

Qua*l*itative researchers look at data (literally) differently:
• The first difference is that in qua*l*itative research we may be interested in the patterns on the surface of the rough stone. We may consider these natural patterns to be of more intrinsic value than any enhancement, amplification or exploitation of the qualities of the stone through *artificial* treatments.

• The next difference is that in qua*l*itative research we will wish to use treatments which involve humans as the instruments of treatment, rather than mechanistic tests or numerical models. We want the data treatments to be of humans and by humans, since it is these qualities in the data which we value and wish to preserve through congruent treatment.

• The third difference is that in qua*l*itative research we do not say that the *process* of the treatment is just as important as the outcome. *We understand that the process is the outcome*. The process of treating data **is** the process of discovering meaning in the data and since it is human researchers that have chosen and implemented the treatment, we are simultaneously making, discovering and describing the meaning in the data.

• The final difference is that in qua*l*itative research we are looking for patterns and qualities, not numbers and quantities. In order to achieve this we may have to consider putting data together to *synthesise* meaning rather than take the data apart into ever smaller units to *analyse* meaning. This is a little like those pictures made up of dots that make no sense when you stand close to them. In order to see the meaning in the pattern, you have to first of all turn your back on the picture, walk a long way from it, screw up your eyes and look at it with half closed eyelids. Then you see the pattern. In qua*l*itative data analysis, we try what might seem to be rather disconnected or bizarre ways of treating data. The common sense which they all bring is that they each try to use a uniquely human attribute or aptitude in order to bring out or discover the meaning inherent in the data.

These differences are variations on the technology-nature dimension (mentioned on page 2). On this dimension the difference between qua*nt*itative and qua*l*itative methods is the difference between believing that we can (only) advance through technology, or on the other hand that we cannot enhance nature through artificial processes, all we do is destroy it.

The questions to consider are:
• *What is data?*
• *Should data treatment be natural, human and congruent with the data, or does it need treatment with special statistical instruments to reveal the order inherent in it?*
• *How can we best express this congruence in the way we treat our data?*

Purpose of research

You would be forgiven for thinking that there is only one purpose of research - to discover the truth. Not an unreasonable assumption, but nevertheless one that on checking turns out to be a little short of the mark. The point about the debate between qua*l*itative and qua*nt*itative philosophies is that one side acts as though truth exists in some absolute form, that there is obviously only one way of discovering truth and that any suggestion otherwise is heresy. This is the qua*nt*itative version that we have all grown up with.

The philosophical position underpinning qualitative approaches suggests that truth is a socially constructed notion and therefore variable depending upon your point of view. (Even some research physicists now take this line.) So what then can the purpose of research be if there is no absolute truth? *It is to seek an understanding of the contexts of truths.* Where the quantitative researcher seeks the small truth from a limited sample in order to generalise it to the big truth of the population, the qualitative researcher seeks to contextualise the truths. Only by understanding the context can we understand the viewpoint of the actors in the context which generated the view of truth and so come to some tentative explanation.

The questions to consider are:
* *What is the purpose of research?*
* *Is it to generalise from small samples to populations, make predictions and find causal explanations or to create and understand contexts, understanding the perspectives of others and understanding the part our collection and treatment of that data has played in the final explanations?*

Qualitative work and counselling

The challenge presented by qualitative research is to let go of our notions that facts are important and that the only things worth knowing are discovered by controlling variables, counting things and applying logic to the numbers. Imagine if you can, a subjective, process-oriented research in which feelings are felt and then subjected to a process of chaotic synthesis.

The words used in qualitative research are words we use to indicate human processes because the human researcher with all of their wonderfully complicated influences is put at the heart of the research process. In quantitative approaches the human factors are excluded as far as possible because they are thought to contaminate the outcome. Qua*l*itative research is of people, about people and done by people.

In this book, we will use our understanding of counselling approaches to help our understanding of a qua*l*itative approach to research methods wherever possible. Counselling approaches can be thought of in terms of several 'dimensions' similar to the ones listed on page 2. Some are more subjective, intuitive, unstructured and person-centred, whilst others are more objective, structured, fact and natural science-centred.

Most counsellors will be familiar with the philosophical, theoretical and practical bases of behavioural counselling and person-centred counselling, and the consequent differences between them. We will use these two approaches to counselling to illustrate the different approaches to research. Some researchers and readers might think that the analogy has limited use and we welcome the debate. If readers start thinking about and debating the issues in this way, the analogy will have achieved its first objective.

A behavioural approach to counselling and person-centred counselling can occupy the two poles of a continuum, with many degrees of difference and combination of ideas and practice between them, yet their basic philosophies remain fundamentally and exclusively different. We have set out some of these differences in this first chapter, some are of the *fundamental* kind, some are more flexible and might indicate areas of compromise.

Where do you stand on these issues as they are presented?
What concepts do you see as fundamental to your belief system?
What ideas of your own are missing from this list (it is not intended to be comprehensive)?

Behavioural counselling	Person-centred counselling
•Learning processes are responsible for change. •Feelings can be manipulated by thoughts. •Observable behaviour is of prime importance. •Logical rational processes are thought to guide behaviour and mental life. •External frame of reference is used. •Measurable elements are behaviour are sought and quantified in order to evaluate change. •Empirical/pragmatic approach to effectiveness of therapy - if it works, use it. •The 'person' is thought of as a 'behaviour machine' or sometimes even a black box, the contents and workings of which are less important than the outcome, i.e. the behaviour. •Trust in the scientific principles of learning gives this method its power and integrity.	•The human tendency towards purposeful, positive self fulfilment is responsible for change. •Experiences are of prime importance. •Logic and rationality are not important in the understanding of people. Persons each have their unique logic. •The internal frame of reference is used. •Only that which the person sees as important is used, whether it be behaviour or experience, measurable or not. Measurement is not seen as important. •The person determines what is important. •The person is seen as central to the process, enigmatic and autonomous, wise and powerful. •Trust in human processes of change gives this method its power and integrity
Behaviourism	**Person-centred humanism**

Practitioners occupying the extreme poles of these methods, approach the whole process of counselling and personal change in fundamentally different ways. Researchers occupying the extreme poles of research methodology approach the whole process of data collection and analysis in fundamentally different ways.

• A behavioural counsellor looks at the client objectively in the same way as the quantitative researcher tries to distance themselves from the process of research in order to become an objective, neutral data collector.
• A behavioural counsellor deals in measurable, quantifiable behaviour in the same way that a quantitative researcher does.
• A behavioural counsellor applies the laws of learning in the same way that a quantitative researcher applies the laws of empirical science.

On the other hand
• A person-centred counsellor will put the client at the centre of the process, just as the qualitative researcher does.
• The person-centred counsellor sees the change process as a relationship event, just as the qualitative researcher sees research as a relationship between the researcher and the things being researched.
• The person-centred counsellor will trust and follow the client's process in the same way that the qualitative researcher trusts and follows the research process - wherever it may lead.
• The Person-centred counsellor understands that the self of the therapist is an integral part of the process and must enter the relationship congruently, just as the qualitative researcher needs to understand their own self and their role in the process of research.

This analogy can be developed further. Perhaps you don't agree with some of the statements above, or you might like to see how far it goes before it starts to break down. Either way we have found it a useful tool in understanding some of the issues at the heart of the qualitative/quantitative debate. Behavioural and person-centred counsellors follow these paths because they believe in different models of humankind and human change processes. These differences follow us into the world of research too. Those who follow a humanist, person-centred philosophy would generally seek to carry it into research. They believe that people-research should put people and people-processes at its centre. Attempts to control, quantify, measure or objectify the person distort the elements under study to such a degree as to make the research invalid.

Of course, it is not only person-centred counsellors who seek a method of research that is congruent with their world-view. The principles of qualitative research are not exclusively person-centred. The analogy we have used may give that impression, but as you read on it will become clear that some of the debates in research methodology are about developing methods of study which are congruent with the philosophical bases of therapeutic approaches, rather than hostile or damaging to them or that, of necessity, make them invalid as a consequence of the data collection process.

- The first question a beginning researcher interested in studying counselling or psychotherapy should ask themselves is,
  'What therapeutic approach do I want to ask questions about?'

- And then,
  'What theoretical and philosophical assumptions regarding the nature of humankind and the change process underpin it?'

- Finally,
  'What way of studying it would be at least congruent with it and perhaps even enhance it?'

You don't have to be an expert on research methods to come to some sort of useful answers to these questions. Many of us have already found our natural leaning in terms of therapeutic approaches. We feel a resonance or harmony with certain ways of doing things. Sometimes we go along with this leaning and sometimes we deliberately go in another direction to challenge the cosy, comfortable feelings of merely confirming our prejudices. Wherever you stand on this you will have a sense of how you prefer to do things, how you prefer to study and discover important 'truths'.

From this starting point you have taken your first step in qualitative research; you have considered yourself and your place in the process - your 'method' if you like. In the following chapters we will look at some popular qualitative methods and some guidelines and principles to follow to make sure you get your own method as valid as you want it to be.

Compare and Contrast #1

Consider the following three examples of study, in which people come to grips with finding something out. Each starts with a problem or question which an individual or group wish to have answered.

1
Janet, a college counsellor, was interested to notice that each year, during enrolment, there was a stream of anxious, disoriented new students arriving at the counselling service. Whilst this was 'good for business' and made her yearly figures look good, she was sure that the college should be able to help these students more but she wasn't sure how. She thought it was important to see what the students felt about it themselves. At the beginning of every academic year she visited classes to talk about the counselling service, so when she visited the English department she asked the staff to help in her project. They agreed and got the students to write a story about arriving at college, based on what it was like for them. The staff then asked the students to write another story based on a perfect first week at an ideal college. Finally, the staff got the student group to make written recommendations to the college principal on how to improve the college 'welcome' to new students.

2
On arriving at her new job as psychology lecturer, Aysha was appalled to find that the college had no counselling service and no plans to start one. She wanted to marshal evidence to persuade the college management that a counselling service was indeed needed. She wrote to all the other colleges in the region to find out how many had counselling services and of what type. She devised questionnaires for staff, students, parents and employers to

find out whether a counselling service would be seen as an asset and whether students thought they would benefit from having someone to talk over their personal problems with. Finally, Aysha tabulated all her results and presented them in a written paper for the academic board.

3
Another psychology lecturer at a neighbouring college, also without a counselling service, found that in his role as personal tutor, students were coming to him with their problems. Sometimes he felt completely out of his depth and would worry at night about whether he was handling the situation well. Whilst realising that a college counselling service could be the answer, he wasn't sure how to find out about counselling nor how best to convince the senior management. He put a notice up in the staff common room asking if any other staff encountering the same problem would like to meet to discuss what they should do. Eight other tutors turned up to a meeting and decided to meet as a support group one lunchtime every week. Through talking about the problems that they suffered themselves as a consequence of listening to the problems of others, they got a clearer picture of what was needed in college to support students and the mostly untrained staff who listen. The group decided to invite some senior managers to one of their meetings to find out for themselves exactly what the problem was and how it affected students and staff.

What do you think of these three pieces of 'research'. Did any of them seem more 'real', giving 'hard' data which would be more credible? Did any methods seem more congruent with counselling approaches ? Did any methods 'speak' to you as being more in harmony with your own preferred way of doing things? 1 and 3 are examples of qualitative methods, whilst 2 is an example of a quantitative method.

16 An Incomplete Guide to Qualitative Research Methods

2 Approaching Qualitative Research

Some important questions

All of us who want to do some research, quantitative or qualitative, have our reasons. This chapter will look at how the reasons that we have (some of which we may not have declared or may not even have thought about) affect the research both in terms of what we do and how we do it.

Compare and Contrast #2
(Contexts and Motives)

A quantitative approach does not acknowledge any reasons other than intellectual reasons for making decisions regarding research. In fact such an approach tries to remove all other possible factors such as political motives, personal motives, emotions, issues of identity and background etc. It's as though research is a sterile zone where only intellect rules.

A qualitative approach, on the other hand, attempts to understand the factors which create a context for the research by embracing them all. In fact as qualitative researchers we are behoven to try to identify, declare and acknowledge the possible effects of our motives, origins and identity. Since qualitative research is about humans, by humans and of humans, we would not seek to eliminate the human touch. We must mindfully include it in order to understand it better.

Why am I doing this research?
This is the first and obvious question to ask yourself. Reasons may vary from the positive and personal:
  'Because I was involved in an armed robbery at my bank and I want to find out about support for PTSD in my area.'
  'I've always wanted to do research and this is a wonderful opportunity.'
  'I'm fascinated by the whole area of spirituality and counselling and wanted to find out more.'
To the distant, removed and reluctant:
  'Because my boss told me to do it.'
  'I said I'd do it so I'll keep my word, even though I'm no longer interested.'
Or the pragmatic:
  'Because we have received funding to do this project.'
  'The future of the centre depends upon us being able to show that it's meeting a need.'

• Finding your reasons for research is the first step in calibrating yourself as the research instrument (see Chapter 3 p.35).
• It helps you get a sense of the context in which the research is taking place and the motives for the research.
• The reasons for doing the research will also point you in a certain direction in terms of how you will organise your work. For example, the reason:
  'Because I was involved in an armed robbery at my bank and I want to find out about support for PTSD in my area.'
Might point you in the direction of a case study approach (see p.28), whereas:
  'The future of the centre depends upon us being able to show that it's meeting a need.'
Might point you more in the direction of an evaluative study (see p.31).
• There may be other motives for entering into research activity - political reasons such as interest in developing ideas and findings relating to sexism, racism, and other issues of oppression.

• When pursuing a qualitative approach, this self-inquiry at the beginning of your research work is not preparation for the research - it is the start of the research. Since qualitative research is of humans and by humans, your humanness (as expressed, at least in part, in your reasons for doing the work) become part of it. *Your research has already begun.*

What am I trying to find out?

Discovering and developing your research question is the next crucial stage in your research. There is no formula or approved procedure to follow that will guarantee a research question. There are, however, some pitfalls and obstacles which are best marked on the map so that aspiring researchers can avoid them if they choose. There is always, of course, the time-honoured method of learning by your own mistakes.

Campbell, Daft and Hullin (1982) offer a summary of the process which is well worth reading for beginning researchers. They suggest that successful research arises from:
- involvement with fieldwork and activity
- the convergence of interests, e.g. a person with a problem plus a person with an idea or method for solving it
- a feeling that the time is right or intuition
- good grounding in the theoretical issues
- projects which end up with tangible changes or benefits.

Disappointment is more likely to follow research based on expedience, a need to demonstrate or 'sell' a 'method', or motivation based on 'profit' (money, publication, fame).

A healthy way of proceeding can be developed by adopting a 'humble' approach:
- Don't assume you know everything. Spend some time getting to know the background to the issue you are thinking of researching.
- Search around the area, not just in your narrow area of interest.
- Don't decide too early, be prepared to let ideas come and go; ask yourself why am I holding on to this way of working or thinking.

- Get other people involved - ask for help, seek out others with experience in the area you are interested in.
- Be careful to end up asking a question that can be answered within your means.
- Have someone check your work with a view to putting a brake on over-ambition.
- If you are serious about this project, get someone to supervise your work...now!

How do I want to express myself through this work?
This question is about the extent to which your identity is consciously bound up with your research method. Do the decisions you make about research approach and methods have *congruence with various aspects of your person* at their heart?

You may have already gone some way to answering this question for yourself since you might have already decided that qualitative rather than quantitative approaches resonate more with your personality, or will allow you to express your *self* better through your research.

The answer to this question may also lead to a leaning towards, or wholehearted commitment to, a particular approach to research. If you are a woman, this may mean a desire to embrace the features of feminist approaches to research. You may wish to take an approach to research that is more ethno-sensitive or based in a philosophy more congruent with your cultural background or ethnic origins.

Women's perspectives - feminist research

People interested in the wider contexts of research have been inevitably drawn to ideas relating to perspectives other than the dominant quantitative perspective. One view that originated over twenty years ago and is now well-organised, takes a feminist approach to research. The field of feminist research grew from certain observations about the world of research as it existed twenty years ago and, some would argue, little has changed. Feminist research grew out of an awareness of the following dynamics of

traditional research (for a more extensive descriptive account see Callaway 1981):
- *The absence of women in traditional research* - sadly unsurprising, traditional research in the social sciences has been and largely continues to be dominated by men.
- *Raised awareness of women's issues amongst women* - individually and collectively women have become more autonomous and have found a stronger voice. This has meant that women are more likely to stand up and make themselves heard.
- *Emergence of women's perspectives* - it is argued by some that women have a qualitatively different way of being. This different way of being leads to a different way of constructing and explaining the world, different values and different perspectives.
- *Increase in the perceived validity and value of women's experience* - more and more people are seeing the value of looking at the experience of others, including women. Women's experience is of interest not only to other women but to anyone wishing to synthesise solutions through incorporating diverse experiences.

One of the strong arguments in favour of creating a separate strand of feminist research is that the traditional research paradigm is sexist by its very nature. A less separatist approach, still identifying inherent sexism in traditional research, is put forward by Eichler (1988) who argues for a 'non-sexist' approach and that traditional research is biased in the following ways:
- *Androcentricity*: looking at the world from an exclusively male viewpoint. E.g. by assuming that a method piloted on males will be suitable for use with women, or making assumptions about patterns of availability, work, education, socialisation, etc. that do not acknowledge that things may be different for women.
- *Ignoring gender*: simply forgetting that gender might be an issue by, e.g. failing to report the gender of the protagonists, subjects or actors.

- *Gender stereotyping*: making assumptions about what may or may not be appropriate for each gender, e.g. child rearing is necessarily 'women's work' or fire-fighting is necessarily a male activity.
- *Overgeneralisation*: when a study generalises from a single sex sample to all the population (both sexes). E.g. a study of abused women drawing conclusions about the behaviour and symptoms of all victims.
- *Double standards*: the flip-side of overgeneralisation is when a study treats men and women participants differently for spurious or unacknowledged reasons.

As researchers interested in qualitative approaches we are behoven to listen to, and take account of, these views. One response might be to avoid the mistakes listed above in our own research. It is, however, not just a matter of developing an 'anti-sexist checklist' for your research project. It is necessary to develop and internalise an awareness of how our backgrounds and experiences bring certain ways of looking at the world, understanding our experience and working. We might then see how we are limited as researchers and how our work might be enriched by broadening our perspectives. Of course it is not possible to take one's perception beyond our experiences, for example men cannot take a women's perspective. This applies to the issues raised below regarding ethnocentricity in research (see p.24).

Finally, it is worth recording that we two white, middle-class, able bodied, heterosexual males are the least qualified to write with any authority on the subject of alternative perspectives. We happily acknowledge the valuable and positive contribution made by the feminist approaches to research, and would encourage all those interested to read more and become involved.

Others have pointed out the positive contribution that feminist research can make to human understanding because of the inherently different ways in which women understand the world and their

experience. Mary Gergen (1988) suggests that feminist research pursues the following themes:
1. *Recognising the interdependence of experimenter and subject.*
2. *Avoiding the decontextualisation of the subject or experimenter from their social or historical settings.*
3. *Recognising and revealing the nature of your values within the research context.*
4. *Accepting that facts do not exist independently of their producer's linguistic codes.*
5. *Demystifying the role of the scientist and establishing an egalitarian relationship between science makers and science consumers.*

This list might, in 1994, be seen as an adequate manifesto for qualitative research in general. Although some might argue about where the influences originated, feminism, sociology, humanism or general discontent with traditional research, it is clear that there is considerable harmony between the themes of the qualitative approach and the feminist approach. We say *the* feminist approach, but of course there is no *single* feminist approach and there is much debate amongst those that own a feminist influence in their work.

Sexist language: Counsellors will know of the importance of language in both personal development and interpersonal relationships. Recently there has been a backlash against what is being called 'political correctness', and much of value has been lost in the media splashes. Both the British Psychological Society (BPS) and the British Sociological Association (BSA) produce guidelines on anti-sexist language, [see, e.g. BSA (1989a), and BSA (1989b)] produce similar guides looking at anti-racist language. If you are concerned about language use or are keen to make sure that your use of language is acceptable to professional organisations, you should refer to one of the above documents.

Ethnocentricity in research

Ethnocentricity is defined by Banyard and Hayes (1994) as:
'Being unable to conceptualise or imagine ideas, social beliefs or the world, from any viewpoint other than that of one's own particular culture or social group. The belief that one's own ethnic group, nation, religion....is superior to all others.'
p.130.

The issue here is how to acknowledge and embrace our ethnicity in our research without becoming ethnocentric. The criticism of traditional approaches is that it is centred around white Euro-American culture and fails to include other cultural perspectives. The issues that arise from this critique are essentially similar to those raised by feminist researchers - see above pp.21 & 22 - and the remedy is essentially the same, e.g:

• Realise the limitations of looking at the world from one exclusive viewpoint.
• Include diverse perspectives wherever possible and appropriate.
• Remember that race and culture are always an issue - have this as a 'standing item' on your personal agenda.
• Do not fall into the trap of cultural, ethnic or racial stereotyping.
• Do not overgeneralise - unless you have a multi-ethnic, multi-racial or multi-cultural sample, generalisation is limited and must be acknowledged as such.
• Do not make the mistake of thinking that 'people are all the same' and therefore must be treated equally. Acknowledge, respect and celebrate the differences through your research.
• Do not operate double standards in your research.

Racist Language: See 'Sexist Language' p.23.

Ways of organising your research
When you have discovered what the topic of your research will be, and what elements of yourself (past experiences, personality, identity) you want to express through your work, you will then turn to how you are going to organise your work. Much of the question asking and answering that has gone on so far in this chapter will have taken you further forward in terms of suggesting more-or-less sensible ways of organising your research. We hope that this section will help you understand some global or umbrella methods of organisation. Put simply you need to decide what *kind* or *type* of study you want to conduct.

All studies are...
It would be convenient to be able to say that underneath it all there is some principle of organisation that binds together all qualitative research. Unfortunately this is not the case. We can, however cheat a little for the sake of making a point about organisation by saying that a research project should be organised in a way that enables and is congruent with, what it is trying to achieve.

It would be true to say that unless you are deliberately trying to replicate someone else's study, no two ways of organising a study are the same. There are, however, some fundamental templates which we can use to see how we might best organise our work:
• If you are trying to prove something, you would choose an *empirical* or *experimental* method, usually quantifying the experiences along the way.
• If you are comparing two or more things (experiences, measures or whatever) then your method will be *comparative* or *correlational*.
• If you are wanting to gather together the stories of a number of people, you will be *surveying* their experience.
• If you are wishing to *evaluate* something, your method will limit itself to including only that which you are seeking to evaluate.
• If you are seeking to elaborate or contextualise the experience of individuals or a group, then your method will confine itself to exploration of the *case* or *cases* in question.

This leads us to a limited number of ways of organising research work:
Experiment (not a qualitative method and therefore not covered in this book - see Sanders and Liptrot 1993 pp102-114).
Correlation (again a largely (though not exclusively) quantitative method covered in Sanders and Liptrot 1993 pp116-122).
Survey* - usually more quantitative than qualitative.
Evaluation study* - can be qualitative or quantitative method.
Case study* - the main form of meta-organisation of qualitative work.
* All covered in this book on the following pages.

Compare and Contrast #3
(Size)

One of the dimensions on which qualitative and quantitative research generally differs is size. Size, that is, of sample.

Since quantitative methods are seeking to generalise their findings from a sample to the population from which the sample was drawn, the sample must be representative of the population both in terms of its constitution and its size. This means that quantitative researchers are after the largest sample they can get (bearing in mind certain statistical factors such as the law of diminishing returns.) In most quantitative studies, big is beautiful for the additional reason that a large sample distributes any errors over a wider area.

Qualitative approaches, however are trying to contextualise experience rather than generalise findings. This change in the nature of the activity has implications for all aspects of the organisation of the work. Since the aim is to understand contexts or narratives then the study can only get so big before the context becomes invalid or meaningless. So generally in qualitative research, small is beautiful. This means that we are generally working with small numbers of participants or actors and we are more interested in the quality of the experiences than the number of them.

Surveying the data: Most readers will, when confronted with the word 'survey' immediately think of being accosted in the high street by a clipboard wielding market-research-survey person. We are not using the term survey in that narrow sense here. Rather we mean to point out that one way of planning your data seeking activities is to see the activity as *surveying experience*. The particular defining factors are:
• The people you are surveying will not belong to the same group.
• Although not belonging to the same group, they may have some common strand of experience which you are interested in, i.e. all having been bereaved in the past six months.
• On some occasions, the only common strand in their lives is that you have chosen them at random to take part in your study.
• You will usually have one contact with them or data collection episode. (On occasions you may follow up with a further contact.)
Note: If you are collecting data from a very small group or from all members of a cohesive, naturally occurring group with many common strands of experience, then your study might be more like a case study.

Once you have decided upon a survey, you will choose a data collection method. The methods most suited to surveys are interrogation and exploration, or questionnaires and interviews. (Full accounts of these methods are given on pp.88-106.) This does not mean, however that other methods are ruled out - you may, for example, want to *survey* the environmental health reports for the past ten years; the data collection issues are still largely the same.

One further question remains and that concerns how you *sample* the data. You don't have to be a hard-line quantitative researcher to be interested in sampling. You should always be prepared to ask yourself 'Why did I choose these people, this group, these records?' etc. Indeed, this may be the most relevant and vital point in your method, without a full account of which, the whole point of the study is lost. You then have to ask yourself 'Which, out of all these possible questions, are the ones I will ask?' This way of looking at sampling is well suited to qualitative analysis, since we are more concerned with the meaning of the decisions than the numbers which are defining the samples.

If sampling concerns you or you think you need to know more, see Sanders and Liptrot (1993) pp.70-76. In qualitative work, it is acceptable to sample in any way you choose, as long as you acknowledge the method you have chosen. Picking your friends and relations is fine if this method has some bearing on the study and you can give a thoughtful and considered account of why.

Case Studies: The main qualitative method is called a case study. Case studies make a major contribution to our knowledge and understanding of human processes for a number of reasons:
• A well researched case study that contradicts an existing theory, however previously well-validated, can raise serious questions against the theory. Well-established ideas have been seriously undermined by good case study evidence.
• Case studies have been seminal in the development of understanding, e.g. the work of Freud (treatment of hysteria), Piaget (stages of intellectual development in children), Osgood (multiple personalities) and other psychologists is based on seminal case studies.
• Our understanding of human processes would be very cold and dry without the detail and warmth contributed by the personal dimension of case studies. This is particularly true of our understanding of human distress, where case studies give a deeper insight into suffering: most counsellors will be familiar with Virginia Axline's (1964) case study reported in *Dibs: In Search of Self*.

Some books refer to different *types* of case study, but we will simply give you some pointers to how a case study might be organised, what data might be included and leave the rest to your creativity.

You may organise a case study around:

- One individual.
- A naturally-occurring group of individuals - this could be a community, a family, or an organisation for example.
- A specially constructed group of individuals - a self-help group convened for the purposes of the study.
- An event - a disaster or crisis, a social occasion such as a wedding or funeral.
- A relationship or set of relationships - a particular counsellor-client relationship, or the counsellor-supervisor relationships in a certain student counselling service.
- Roles - 'the counsellor' role or counsellor/teacher role conflicts.

Note: If your group is very large, or the individuals do not have strong common strands, or you end up having to sample the people in some way, then the study might be more like a survey.

'What does a case study look like?' or 'How do you know if you're doing a case study?' are reasonable questions, since it could be argued (as we have said elsewhere) that all qualitative work is case study work. A case study (simply) involves collecting information about an individual person or discrete, identifiable (small) group. The same general principles of research need to be followed when conducting a case study, as are followed in other forms of research. For example, understanding and describing any theoretical background; locating the study in a context in the real world; finding a baseline; looking for, describing or measuring change; accounting for, explaining or interpreting the findings; referring back to theory.

Case studies can be approached in a more-or-less systematic and structured way. The following steps may be of use if you are unfamiliar with case studies or unsure how to proceed. We will assume that you have done all the necessary work on finding and developing your research question.

- Identify the subject of your case study (individual, group or whatever).
- Is there a theoretical background to the work you are planning?
- Take a case *history* - this will help describe the real world context of the case and find a baseline (if necessary).
- When is the case study set in time? Case studies can be:
  - retrospective - describing events that have already happened and are being re-visited, remembered or reviewed.
  - present and ongoing - describing events happening now.
  - forward-looking - setting up a situation to describe future events, e.g. setting up a case study to describe the early bonding experiences of your as-yet unborn child.
- Select a data collection method (see below) and collect the data.

Freud used a case-study approach to describe his work with patients, and case study method has, for years been an accepted way of presenting clinical work and clinical findings. The discrete 'group' referred to earlier could be, for example, a group of clients with a similar presenting problem, or a family group, etc. whose clinical records are presented in case study format.

Do not, however, be mesmerised by the clinical case presentation style that may be familiar to you. This will only limit the opportunities for data collection, treatment and presentation. Although case studies are essentially simple descriptions of events, there are no real rules regarding how the material described should be collected or presented. Often case studies are presented in a chronological sequence, but this is not a requirement. If you feel a different form of presentation suits your collection method or data treatment better, then use it.

When conducting a case study, it really is open season as far as data collection methods are concerned. There is no 'not recommended' category of data collection in a case study, in fact the one suggestion we would make is to encourage you to use as wide a variety of methods as time, money, energy and other resources permit. The only warning note is to keep within realistic limits - don't collect a mountain of data that overwhelms you when it comes to data analysis.

Although having a *plan* regarding how you are going to sample the data in your study is necessary, sampling itself is not such a burning issue in the average case study as it is in a survey. This is usually either because of the small numbers involved or because you will be 'sampling' all of the actors' behaviour, thoughts and feelings. You will not be limiting your data collection to a small sub-set of information or from a small sub-set of people within the group.

- If you are doing a case study on an individual, you may have to sample their behaviour, thoughts or feelings in some way - it would be difficult to record their behaviour, etc. 24 hours a day.
- If you are doing a case study on a group, family, community, or organisation, it may be difficult to record data from each individual, and again, it will prove impractical to record data 24 hours a day, 7 days a week.
- The method you choose to record a portion of the data for only a portion of the time is your sampling method. Your sampling decisions are:
  - Who will you collect data from?
  - What data are you going to collect?
  - When will you collect it?
  - Where will you collect it?
- For more on sampling see Sanders and Liptrot (1993)p.70.

Evaluation Studies: The idea of evaluating something will be familiar to most readers. All of us have, at least intuitively, tried to evaluate the effectiveness of our counselling practice at some time or another. Occasionally we may be asked to evaluate the effectiveness and/or the efficiency of a counselling service. Although effectiveness and efficiency have become bywords for evaluation in the late 80s and early 90s, there are other themes that can be the subject of evaluation. Here are a few examples, the list is not exhaustive:

Effectiveness	Efficiency
Feasibility	Adequacy
Appropriateness	Usefulness/utility
Legality	Ethics
Validity	Reliability
Trustworthiness	Benefit
Quality	Cost

These evaluative themes can be pursued at different times in the *life-cycle* of a particular event. Looked at in this way, we can see a use for evaluation before, during and after an event or intervention.
• Evaluation of the situation before something is started, e.g. feasibility studies. *Asking the questions, 'Is it worth doing?' or 'Will it work?'*
• Evaluation of the changes in something as it happens, e.g. developmental analysis. *Asking the questions, 'How is it doing?' or, 'How is it changing?'*
Evaluation of the process of something as it happens, e.g. process evaluation or monitoring. *'Asking the question, 'What is happening?'*
• Evaluation of the effect or impact of something, e.g. outcome analysis. *Asking the questions, 'Was it worth doing?' or, 'Did it work?'*

Once you have decided what you are evaluating, for what purpose and at what time in the life-cycle of an event, there are still some matters to resolve before you can start collecting data. Remember that an evaluation study is essentially comparative. In other words it is comparing whatever is being evaluated to a standard of some sort. It might be a norm of some description ('acceptable behaviour') or an absolute standard (e.g. set by legislation) or one you make up yourself. When planning your evaluation you might consider the following:

- Do you need permission to get access to documents, areas, personnel?
- Are you evaluating something against criteria or against some absolute idea or reference point?
- Do you need and have you got a baseline measure?
- If you are using criteria, are you using someone else's criteria or are you generating your own?
- If you are generating your own criteria, what criteria are you using to evaluate against?
- Who wants this work done - you or is someone commissioning it?
- How will the findings be used - will you have the final say, or will someone else?
- If someone else is commissioning this work, how do they want it written up or presented?

When you have addressed all of the above issues to your satisfaction you will be at the stage of considering data collection. As with case studies, the field is open as far as data collection is concerned. Any appropriate method can be used and there is much to be said for using a variety of methods. Documents, interviews, questionnaires, participant observation and others all have a valid contribution to make to an evaluation study.

Finally you will have to have some sort of strategy when it comes to sampling. Much the same considerations apply to evaluation work as apply to case studies, see p28. In fact your evaluation study may well be a case study with a particular purpose or aim, i.e. evaluation.

3 Preparing for Qualitative Research

Calibrating your instrument.
You may have become used to regarding your body as a temple. Now is the time to alter that perception. As a researcher using qualitative methods, your body is an instrument (and so is your mind). As with other instruments, the more finely it is tuned, the better it will perform. Much of the success of your research will depend on the amount, type and appropriateness of your preparation.

The idea of self-calibration in qualitative research is similar to the idea of self-awareness development in counselling. The qualitative researcher needs to be more than a little self-aware so that their own tendencies, attitudes, ways of seeing things, etc. are acknowledged and accounted for as factors contributing to the findings. Counsellors will be familiar with the notion of becoming aware of their own attitudes, feelings and thoughts in preparation for being an effective counsellor. This should make counsellors into good qualitative researchers, as long as we follow some simple guidelines:
- Examine your motives, personal, professional, financial. How will these colour your thinking?
- Are you out to prove a point? What ideas are you trying to advance under the guise of research?
- What are your anxieties? Will you turn away from certain findings?
- Make sure you have someone to turn to check out your thinking on this research - get supervision.
- Keep a personal journal.

The following sections will consider aspects of preparation for conducting your research. However, the sections are not intended to be viewed as a chronological plan. Some of the aspects of the planning will be in operation simultaneously, and others will require consideration on different occasions during the planning stage of the research.

Literature review

Whatever the scale of your proposed study, there will inevitably be some background reading to be done. There are several functions that this reading will perform. These include:
• Establishing the background against which your research will be set - what have other researchers in the area discovered, or what have other theorists proposed.
• Using this information to support the findings that you obtain or use the existing work as a starting point for your research with the intention of adding to the body of work, or arguing with the present state of thinking.
• Referring to the work of others may give ideas as to how your work should or should not be conducted and contribute ideas on methods of data analysis, selection of people or situations to work with, etc.

It is unlikely that the work that you are proposing is entirely unique, or that work relevant to your proposal does not already exist. It is probable that you will be required to show evidence of having researched the literature currently available, and use this to place your work in a context and demonstrate how it relates to that which already exists. Of course the depth and breadth of the literature review will largely be dependant on the nature of, or reason for, your study and hopefully you will have been given guidelines as to what is expected of you.

Obtaining your material
For the most part, you will be obtaining your material from two main sources - books and journal articles. Other sources that may be of use, depending on the nature of your research project, will be

theses, annual reports, magazine and newspaper articles (particularly those in specialist titles). There will be a bewildering array of possible sources of information available in all of these sources and before proceeding with a search through the available material it will be necessary, not only to have selected the topic for which you are searching, but also to have defined exactly what you are looking for.

The constraints of time have been mentioned or alluded to on a number of occasions, and here again this may be an issue. Not only will you have to find your sources, but having identified possible sources you will also have to obtain them. The better prepared you are for your literature search, the more effective and less time consuming it will be. The other time related issue is knowing when to give up the literature search - you don't just have to find the material, you also have to read it (and take notes).

Assuming that your research is in some way counselling based - simply searching for counselling related material will yield a vast amount of unnecessary information. However, if you attempt to be too specific, then you may well end up with little or nothing of relevance. For example, searching only for information listed under 'Nurse's perception of counselling' will not produce the desired amount of sources. Listing possible search terms (or descriptors) should help in your task, for example, besides counselling you may wish to add nurses, hospitals, health, all of which may give potential leads.

You may also wish to define the parameters of your search, are you interested in all material relevant to your topic, or only the most recent? Are you only interested in British sources of information? Are you restricting your search to books and or journal articles or are other sources to be included?

Unless you are an experienced user of libraries, which is where you will be gleaning most of your information from, it is also worth making the acquaintance of at least one member of the library staff, since you may need some help in locating the sources of information and actually accessing the information. It is also worth noting that many libraries now offer some sort of introductory package in which users learn how to make use of the library facilities.

It is unlikely that you will have reached this stage without reading at least some relevant information - you should have made a note of any authors whose names were referred to in the text you read as this will provide a starting point for your search

Your cover story - uncovered
Although the most obvious issue is that of the consent of the actual people who will be involved in the study, there are others who must also be considered:
- The management of the institution where the research is to occur (perhaps involving an approach to an ethics committee).
- The staff working in the area in which you will be conducting your research.

This may be particularly important if you are conducting your research at a location where you would normally be viewed as a friend or colleague and where on occasions you will be occupying a different role - that of the researcher. In a later section, more attention will be devoted to ethical issues, one of these being the issue of informed consent.

At various stages in the preparation for your research you will be required to provide either a verbal or written statement concerning your research. Although the type and amount of information you will be required to present will vary between situations and individuals, and once again raises the ethical consideration of deception.

One way to approach the question of what information should be provided is to put yourself in the position of those who you are approaching, institutions or potential subjects, what information would *you* require before granting your permission to be included in a research study? The chances are that you will require a mixture of information and reassurance - what is being done, why is it being done, what is expected of me, and what safeguards do I have? Since qualitative research is congruent, open, respectful, involving and collaborative - honesty is not so much the *best* policy as the *only* one recommended for use in qualitative work - even if it were not required by ethical guidelines. Any hint of deception would distort your relationship with the participants in your study and therefore distort your findings.

Your cover story should not be a cover story in the way a spy has a 'cover story' to conceal the true purpose of their mission, but rather like the cover on a book - giving a honest impression of the contents. Glesne and Peshkin (1992) suggest that all cover stories should address the following points.
• Who you are.
• What you are doing.
• Why you are doing it.
• What will be done with the results.
   Ask the participants what they would like to see happen with the results.
• How the location and subjects were chosen.
• What are the possible benefits and risks to participants.
   Ask the participants if there are any you haven't thought of.
• The promise of confidentiality and anonymity to participants (and organisation if appropriate).
   Don't make promises you can't keep.
• How often and for how long subjects will be required to participate.
   Make a realistic estimate here - don't make their involvement sound less that it really is going to be.
• Requests to record information - and a statement of what methods of recording are intended.
   Make sure you have the right permissions - see gaining access on page 40.
• Clarification that the intention of the researcher is that of understanding rather than judgement.
   This should not be difficult for counsellors.
• Clarification that there are no right and wrong answers or ways of being or behaving and that you intend to learn from them.

As mentioned earlier, the degree to which these points are expanded on will depend on the role of the individual you are dealing with at a particular time. Additionally, be prepared for requests for further information, particularly relating to what feedback can be expected from the researcher. Will participants (institutions or individuals) have access to the results of the study? If you are dealing with people at a distance, for example postal questionnaires, it may be worth including some reference to this at an early stage.

You will of course be faced with the dilemma of exactly how precisely you describe the intentions of your research. Obviously there should be no deliberate intention to mislead anyone regarding the purpose of your study, but there will also be the need to consider the degree to which prior knowledge may influence the behaviour of the participants. As yet another rule of thumb, the best policy may be to give an initial general statement of intent, which may become progressively more specific as the study develops, particularly as piloting of the study may cause a shift in focus. It should go without saying that a copy of your cover story should be included in your proposal, see page 50.

Gaining access

Having decided where you intend to carry out your research, and who with, you may now be faced with the problem of gaining access. The degree to which this may be a difficulty will depend to some extent on your relationship with the institution within which you intend to carry out your research; this may be a reason for conducting your research at the place where you work.

Your cover story may also prove to be of considerable importance in gaining the access you require as it will set out the important elements of your research for consideration by whatever authorities will make the decision.

In the case where you will be conducting research within an institution of which you are not already a member, one problem may be identifying the channels through which access may be gained.

This is another occasion in which consultation with other people may be of benefit. If you are familiar with people within the institution then they may be able to offer help or guidance to identify the channels through which access may be gained.

It is also worth remembering that the wheels of institutions may grind exceeding slow and that the process of gaining access may add considerably to the time required to conduct your study. As an example of a worst case scenario (other than being refused access) the current writer remembers waiting 8 months for a quorate meeting of the committee that could grant the permission he sought!

Location of research
Presumably, the vast majority of readers will already be involved in counselling, or a counselling related activity, and research forms an additional element to this role. A further presumption is that your research interest has developed out of the counselling role that you play. If we are to be allowed a further presumption, it will be that the proposed site of your research will be related to your current field of operation, i.e. you will be playing the role of practitioner-researcher. If you have not yet decided upon the location of the research, you have a wider set of decisions to make (see, for example, gaining access page 40) and even if the location is already decided, it is worth looking in more detail at the advantages and disadvantages of this choice.

Advantages: The majority of the advantages of conducting research within a known location are fairly obvious. The routes for obtaining access are more likely to be well known, and are likely to take less time to negotiate:
- Rapport between the researcher and other participants is likely to be well established.
- The existing social network will also provide great opportunities for support and advice.
- Conducting research within the work location, even if it has not been requested by the organisation, may have personal and professional benefits.

Disadvantages: It may be argued that researching in a familiar environment will aid the research process by providing insights and ideas, both for the actual data collection itself and for the most appropriate methods of investigation. However, others may consider that the experience of researching in the work-setting will cause problems due to previous relationships and expectations that may be difficult if not impossible to work around. Additionally, there is also the problem of switching roles from practitioner to researcher - not only for the researcher themselves, but also in relation to work colleagues and clients.

Allied to the above are ethical and political considerations. On occasions the researcher will be acting as observer; there is the question of how explicit this transition should be, should the researcher wear a green hat whenever they are acting as observer and a different coloured one at all other times? It may also be the case that, in the course of the research, information or practices that are undesirable or unethical may come to light - the reporting of these may have severe consequences, whilst the non-reporting may have equally severe, but different consequences. In brief, the researcher-practitioner may become compromised as a result of the dual role. Finally there is the difficulty in maintaining confidentiality when compiling the final report of the research.

If a decision is made to choose a location external to the normal working environment, the situations are more or less reversed. The advantages of the first situation become disadvantages, whilst the disadvantages of the practitioner-researcher situation become advantages when the researcher has only one role. The initial stages of the research may take longer, but the objectivity and ethical considerations are less likely to be problematic.

Whatever the reasons for choice of location, these should be explicitly stated within the research proposal, including the criteria for location choice. The choice of location will also tie in with the selection of people to work with.

Choosing people to work with

Since generalisation from a sample to a population is not a strong concern for qualitative researchers, we will not consider sampling for the purposes of generalisation here. Even for qualitative research, sampling still remains the best way of limiting your field of study from all of humankind down to the people or person with whom you want to work. This may be achieved through random selection, selecting a stratified sample that matches the characteristics of the population, or using a convenience or opportunity sample - details in Sanders and Liptrot (1993) pp.70-76.

In qualitative work, however you choose the people you want to work with, your rationale must be clearly explained and the criteria for selection made explicit - including reasons why certain people may be excluded from your study, e.g. all people attending a particular service may be considered for inclusion. From this group, individuals will be chosen at random and asked to participate in the study.

It should also be remembered that, if a pilot study is to be conducted (which is desirable if at all possible) then the people used in the pilot should resemble the final selection of people for the study proper as far as is possible, but not the *same* people!

Rapport

Building rapport with those we work with is the stock-in-trade for counsellors. Since much of qualitative work is relationship-based, we will need to pay attention to the manner in which we define our research relationships. They will, of course, be different from our therapeutic relationships, and the quality we want them to have is *rapport*. Rapport is similar but different to the warmth, empathy and genuineness we wish to extend to our clients. It is a matter of definition, intent and boundaries.

The qualities of rapport:
Interest: it is essential to be interested in what the participants
   are doing. Having asked someone to help you in your research
   by giving themselves and their time, there is no place for the

sort of genuineness or congruence we are used to in counselling. Be polite, look happy, be grateful. Occasionally research may put us in contact with disturbed, disturbing or abusive people. It is the researcher's job to try to understand the world of the participant or respondent - not to judge or run away too soon.

Neutrality: Being non-judgemental is an essential quality of rapport. However, we are not required to be *warm* in the therapeutic sense of the word. A polite neutrality is the best attitude to strike.

Respectful boundaries: for more detail on this see 'Your cover story - uncovered' on page 38. Included in this is the idea of confidentiality, which has slightly different connotations in research. There may well be an expectation, on your part at least, that some of what passes between you and the participants or respondents will be published. If this is the case it is imperative that no-one can be identified from the descriptions or quotes that you publish.

Language: use language that will be familiar to your participants or respondents. Do not pretend to be someone or something that you're not. You may have to familiarise yourself with jargon, technical or otherwise specialist words in order to make yourself understood and to understand what is being said to you. This can take some time.

Information: again there is more on this in the 'Your cover story' section on page 38. You must be ready to answer questions as well as give information. Make sure you get the essentials across without boring the other person to death. Your research is interesting to you but not necessarily to anyone else!

Counselling skills: you can and must use your skills in active listening to pay attention and make the discussion feel natural. Remember though, this isn't counselling. You are researching a topic, not being therapeutic. Use your counselling skills to build rapport only.

Trustworthiness

All researchers, qualitative or quantitative are concerned that their findings are trustworthy. What do we mean by this?

Compare and Contrast #4
(Trustworthy findings)

There seems little point in going to all the trouble of planning a study, collecting and interpreting the data for it to be dismissed as untrustworthy. It is a prime concern that our findings be trustworthy and it is a point of difference between qualitative and quantitative methods as to how best to go about establishing this feature.

Quantitative researchers are concerned to establish the reliability and validity of their measurements in the same way that physical scientists do - by taking repeated measures and comparing them to other scientists' measures. Then if the measures look respectably alike (in a numerical sense) they are deemed to be reliable and valid. For more detail on this see Sanders and Liptrot (1993) pages 28-34.

Since qualitative work is about processes, stories and understanding the humanness of being human, it would not be appropriate to seek validity in numbers. Other more naturalistic methods of ensuring that qualitative results are trustworthy must be found. This has proved to be difficult because we are so used to numbers and their historical association with facts (numbers just *are* reliable and trustworthy - after all, two plus two is four). Many of the ways of doing this that have been developed thus far, however, do hark back to physical science methods. Trustworthy human measurement is achieved by:
 • having a well calibrated measuring instrument, see p 35.
 • triangulation*
 • repetition of the measurement, see p.136.
 • analysis of negative cases*
 • participant consultation, see p.137.
*These are covered in the following pages and elsewhere in this book.

Reliability and validity

It is particularly important that the methods you use for collecting information are shown to be both reliable and valid. The reliability of an instrument refers to the degree to which it will produce consistent results. Although there are techniques for establishing the reliability of research instruments in a quantitative setting (see Sanders and Liptrot, 1993), these will not be desirable in qualitative contexts and the issue of reliability may best be addressed through critical appraisal of the choice and implementation of the chosen method.

One question that may be worth considering is the extent to which the same method used again would produce similar results. For example, if the same questions were put to the same subject, would the same response emerge? To a large extent, common sense is a useful tool in this consideration - if the questions were asked at a different time, or under different circumstances, answers may vary considerably - but a reliable instrument or procedure will produce consistent results under the same conditions.

Validity is the more important of the two considerations. A procedure may be reliable without being valid; measuring shoe size will produce consistent results time and time again, but it will tell us nothing about the emotional well being of the respondent. A valid instrument measures what it is intended to measure. A rule of thumb question for considering this aspect of your proposed methodology is to ask, "If another researcher were to use the same procedure as I am, would they obtain the same sort of results?" If the answer is 'No', then your method is likely to lack validity; the results are likely to be a product of your own performance in some way rather than a true reflection of the process, or a particular state, or particular events.

As with other aspects of the planning of your research, the process is not occurring on some uninhabited planet - you have access to other people who will have some insight into the process you are investigating, research methodology, or both. Make use of these people by consulting them whenever possible, practical and desirable. The different perspectives they can supply and the process of consultation itself, will help ensure that your methods are both reliable and valid.

Finally, conducting a pilot study prior to actually conducting the research proper will be of value in assessing the reliability and validity of the procedures you have chosen. It will also reveal any problems with your attempt to apply different techniques to the same situation, should you have decided to include a degree of triangulation.

Triangulation
Whenever I see or hear this term being used, I am immediately torn away from considering research techniques and become lost in a medley of childhood memories in which clean cut heroes of World War II are desperately sending messages by radio from occupied France. At the same time the baddies (for that is what they were in those days) are charging around the countryside in a grey van with a radar on top. They are trying to locate the radio by means of triangulation. They need to locate the radio from two different points to verify its exact location. Without the two readings, the searchers could not be sure whether they have located the correct broadcast site. They may claim to have found it from only one reading, but when they arrive find that their claim was false.

To some extent, when conducting your research, you should look at the possibility of taking on the role of the searchers, by verifying the truth of your claims using two (or more) sets of results, or to enhance the trustworthiness of your data by making use of more than one method of enquiry.

Unfortunately, in small-scale studies, this may prove impractical for a number of reasons, the most obvious being that of time. However serious consideration should be given to both the desirability and possibility of triangulation. For example, the results of observations may be backed up with information derived from a questionnaire administered to some or all of the subjects, or the results obtained from your study may be compared with those previously obtained in similar studies. The use of multiple methods of data collection will enhance the reliability and validity of your findings.

Analysis of negative cases
This simply means looking at your data and attempting to explain why certain cases or findings don't seem to fit into the strong trends, and patterns evident in the majority of cases. Doing this openly, discovering and acknowledging the reasons for the negative cases, gives your readers the opportunity to accept (or otherwise) your interpretation of the findings. Do not cover up or attempt to disguise and results that don't fit. They will always prove to have an interesting story to tell.

Analysis of negative cases establishes trustworthiness by opening the data and its interpretation to a wider scrutiny. Any personal biases will be limited by the research equivalent of 'washing your dirty linen in public' and 'trial by publication'.

Your pilot study
A pilot study should be a vital part of your research planning. The main purpose of your pilot study will not be to collect data or information, but to test or clarify as many aspects of your proposed research as possible.

For example, it is obvious that if you are proposing to use a questionnaire or interview, a significant aspect of the pilot study will be to identify any problems with the questionnaire or interview schedule. However, through this process other problems may emerge that can be dealt with before the study proper. As the pilot study should be as close as possible to the actual study you intend to conduct, the people used in your pilot study should be as similar to the people used in the final study as possible - so the pilot will also help you identify any problems with obtaining persons to work with.

Although ethical aspects of research will be considered later, it should also be made clear to subjects that they are in fact taking part in the piloting of a piece of research rather than the final piece of research itself, though all the other ethical considerations relating to treatment of subjects should obviously still apply.

Practical considerations of the pilot: Perhaps the first question you may ask about your pilot study is how many people should it involve. As the pilot is to be used to fine tune your final study, the main consideration should be that enough people are used to give a real representation of the intended final study and to explore all the problems that are likely to arise - without overdoing it!

• If you are conducting a questionnaire or interview, besides checking that the questions are clear and precise or even necessary, it will also help determine whether the instructions and information given to participants or respondents are clear and sufficient and also to check the time required for conducting or administering the questions. Again, whilst using people that represent your final targets will help answer some of the above questions, such as those concerning the timing and clarity, it will be worth consulting colleagues or supervisors to check on such aspects as appropriateness of questions, and whether there are any important omissions.

• If observational methods are to be used, the pilot will help investigate elements such as; how participants respond to being observed, how well the recording technique operates, are the categories of behaviour being considered comprehensive or realistic?

• Piloting will also help fine tune yourself - are you presenting yourself as you would wish, are there any difficulties in establishing rapport with subjects?

• Finally, conducting the pilot study may also throw up questions that you had not previously considered, and may in fact add or subtract elements to or from the research that had originally been proposed.

Your research proposal

Prior to conducting research, approval will be required in some form. This may be from the organisers of a particular course, from employers or a funding body. In general there will be a required format for the proposal and that should be strictly adhered to. However, it is likely that all proposals will require more or less the same type of information, and this will be addressed later. It may be the case that you look on the writing of a research proposal as an inconvenience prior to conducting the study, but a well-constructed proposal offers many opportunities:

- Firstly, it gives a focus to the planning stages of a project. The proposal will require details of all elements of the proposed work. In turn, this will aid the development of a well-structured piece of research. A frequently used analogy of the research proposal is that of a blueprint. From consideration of the plans, any defects can be identified and corrected before the project commences. Additionally, it will allow consultation with others and viewing from different perspectives, once again offering the opportunity for alterations to be made before they become too costly and time consuming.
- The proposal may also act as an indicator of the competence of the researcher, and its acceptance may therefore be beneficial in terms of the confidence of the researcher - often an issue with first time researchers.
- It should also be remembered that eventually there must be a written report of the research. Much of the preparatory work will be of benefit in producing the final report.

Whatever the purpose of your proposal (academic or professional) and whatever the subject of your proposal, two requirements should predominate, those of clarity and organisation. The intention of your proposal is to inform others of what is intended and will therefore require clear statements of aims and methods. As the research is unlikely to have arisen in a vacuum, the proposal will also have to place the research in some sort of theoretical or situational context (or both). The person who reads the proposal may not necessarily have the some level of knowledge about the topic area that you will have developed through the various stages of the construction of your proposal. They will be seeking clarity of explanation rather than a megalith of jargonistic obfuscation of the main issues masquerading as a demonstration of your academic rigour and prowess!

Whatever structure is used for your proposal, and how much resemblance it has to the proposal format suggested here, the need for organisation is paramount. It should be clear to whoever reads the proposal exactly where particular types of information will be located within the document. The sections should be identified in a clear and consistent manner:

Aims and objectives
Give brief and clear statements of the aims and objectives of the proposed research. You should include a statement of the problem or issue to be investigated. If you feel it is appropriate, you may wish to include a personal statement as to why the particular topic or area has been chosen.

- Unclear objectives or intentions will make it difficult for the research proposal to be assessed positively. You may like to check with others that your statements are clear before submission.
- You should also be clear about the purpose of the research and use your proposal to convince others of its importance or relevance. If others do not consider it important enough, or unlikely to provide new information or perspectives, it is unlikely to be accepted.

Introduction

This section should establish a context for the research - see literature review p 36. Terms should be defined and provide a background to the area under consideration. There should be links to existing theories and reference to previous research. The section should work towards a statement of probable hypotheses or the identification of possible themes that may emerge as the research develops. As with aims and objectives, these should be clear and concise to facilitate positive assessment.

If the research is concerned with a particular organisation, a description of the organisation, identification of its aims and objectives, plus some historical detail will be more appropriate. Though reference may also be made to research concerning similar organisations, should such work exist.

A literature search will be a significant element in preparing your proposal. However, simply proposing a piece of research with no relationship to theory or previous work is unlikely to be accepted.

Methodology

This section will concentrate on the practicalities of the research, how it will be conducted, where, with whom and why.

You should ensure that sufficient detail is provided of all aspects of the way in which you propose to conduct your research. Unless it is clear what is intended, and sufficient detail is provided as to determine the suitability of the chosen method, the proposal is unlikely to be successful. However, the proposed method should be realistic in terms of time, resources and the experience of the researcher. The section should contain sub headings, if appropriate,

Method(s)

Identification and description of research techniques and method(s) to be employed. Reference should be made to the reasons for this choice and to other methods that have been considered but rejected.

People/participants
This section should provide a description of the people chosen for the study, how they were chosen and why.

Location
This section should provide a description and justification of the location(s) at which the study will be conducted.

Materials
This section should begin by listing and/or describing all materials to be used in the study. Where appropriate (e.g. if study involves use of a published questionnaire) the choice of materials should be explained and justified. If any 'home grown' materials are to be used, these should be described, with reference made to their development - including the piloting of the material. This is particularly important in the case of questionnaires and structured or semi-structured interviews.

Data
Provide a description of the type of data that your study will yield and the proposed treatment of the data. Where alternative treatments have been considered and rejected, reference should be made to these. You should not use this section (or any section) to predict the data or results you will achieve.

Ethics
You should provide a review of ethical considerations involved or raised by your study. Where appropriate you should offer an explanation of how ethical issues impact upon the proposal and at what points your decisions may have been influenced by ethical considerations.

Resource considerations
You should also include some appropriate references to financial or time, or other resource considerations associated with your proposed research. This is particularly important if your proposal is to be read by someone who controls funding.

As previously mentioned, you may well have a specified format and a specified number of words (as well as a deadline). These should be adhered to. How long each section will be will vary according to the individual piece of research, so the length of other sections may have to be altered to accommodate this. However, skimping on the amount of information offered, or padding out with unnecessary information are not options that should be considered.

A final point to be remembered is that what you are producing is a proposal - not tablets of stone. As the project unfolds, one or more aspects may change, through interest, development or necessity, so a flexible approach is required. If one aspect of the proposal changes, for example the method or sample of subjects, this may have an effect on other aspects such as the objectives. Flexibility should not be presented as a lack of consistency between aspects of the proposal, a feature which will not enhance the likelihood of acceptance.

Practical considerations

Although the following aspects are less fundamental to the nature and form of your research, they are important considerations that are all too often overlooked during the planning stages of research. There are two main costs to research - time and money. To some extent they can be considered separately, but do overlap to a degree.

Access to resources

Whether you are conducting your research on behalf of an organisation, as a student on a course or as an individual practitioner-researcher, there will be costs involved and these should be considered, particularly if you are to shoulder the burden yourself. You may also wish to look for ways to lighten the load.

A primary cost these days is that of photocopying. In many instances we often take it for granted, but if there is a likelihood that we must pay ourselves then it requires some consideration. If you are copying articles or sections of books for reading other than in the library, firstly check copyright protection, and secondly remember that the costs can mount considerably. If you can't get access to free photocopying, or are required to photocopy on site, plan in advance. It is frustrating to find that you do not have enough money to do the photocopying you require - especially if visits to the library are difficult or infrequent. Do not, as this author has done early in his career, attempt to save money by copying only the text and ignoring the reference sections - this approach required a return to all the original sources to look for further references - a significant waste of time.

The use of questionnaires may also involve much photocopying, or even printing (this can sometimes be cheaper than photocopying). Remember to account for the cost of postage and stationery, especially if you enclose SAEs (a polite and effective way of increasing the response rate). Wherever possible, look for ways of making phone calls at the cheapest possible rates.

Unless you are a skilled typist, it is likely that you will require the services of another person to type the research proposal and final report. Often the format will be specified (typed and double spaced). Not only will this cost money, but will also be a hidden time factor. Not only will the typist require time to produce the document, but it will also require proof reading in order to correct any mistakes, even the best typist is likely to make the odd error.

Speaking as we were of odd errors, if you are typing the report yourself, it is a good idea to enlist the help of a trusted friend (remember confidentiality) to proof read your finished work. It is a truism that we see what we expect to see when we read something we are familiar with, so doing our own proof reading may allow silly mistakes to slip through. Although most word-processing packages now include a spell-check programme, this does not legislate for real words in the wrong context. Your author recently sent a description of conditioning techniques to the publisher with an unwanted reference to *bra pressing* remaining unaltered. Proof reading may often prove to be fertile ground for train spotting Freudians.

Often secretarial staff may be recruited to produce final documents, but it should be remembered that this may not be their official duty, and some appreciation of this would be ethically correct.

If, as is likely, your literature search will involve the use of Inter Library Loans, it is worth remembering that, besides the time element involved, there may be a cost element. It is worth checking with libraries as to what charge if any they make for this facility. The real cost to the library appears to be between £9 and £17. Although you are unlikely to be charged the full amount - it may be worth shopping around if charges are likely. Hopefully your judicious use of abstracts and bibliographies will prevent the ordering of unnecessary items.

Time management
We can regard the research process as containing three major phases - planning, implementation and reporting. Each of these will require time, though to some extent each may run concurrently with another. Inevitably, you will be working to a deadline, and while this may prove to be flexible,it simply means that the time available for other activities also becomes restricted.

In the planning stage, the literature search is likely to take up the bulk of the time required. Remember that you must also read and extract information from the sources you identify. Although the temptation is always there to wait for one more source, it is important to set a deadline and stick as closely as possible to it. Try to be as ruthless as possible, this can be a self-development challenge to many of us pathological perfectionists.

When planning the research, remember that not only is your time involved but also that of others. Besides giving reasonable consideration to others when placing demands on their time, make sure that you are aware of any restraints on their availability. It may appear obvious to readers, but be aware of seasonal variations in the activities of organisations, do not plan to conduct a questionnaire of college staff during the summer.

Wherever possible, negotiate some sort of time allowance with employers that is also recognised by colleagues. This will make it easier to arrange visits or interviews within working hours, any other arrangement may make it difficult to gain access to people.

Be sure to draw up a research timetable. Whatever your timetable looks like, make sure that a degree of flexibility is built in; you cannot legislate for the illness of others, transport difficulties, machinery breakdown, incompatibility of computer equipment etc. It is also worth considering drawing up deadlines after which alternative methods or approaches will be considered rather than sticking to an approach that is obviously becoming unfruitful.

It is also true that your research is unlikely to be as important to others as it is to you and that their full co-operation and immediate attention cannot be guaranteed at all times. Expect the unexpected, the unforeseen disaster and the inevitable frustration and you will only be mildly surprised when it proves to be even worse than that!

Ethical considerations in research

Throughout this book we make repeated references to conducting ethical, principled research. This is true whether you want to do qualitative research or quantitative research. In qualitative work, unethical practice invalidates the process of research because it abuses the relationship between the researcher and the participants which is at the centre of the work. If this relationship loses its integrity, then all is lost. It is not unlike the position of ethics in counselling.

Ethics in Counselling

Some readers will be familiar with the various Codes of Ethics and Practice published by the British Association for Counselling

(BAC). To date they number four; for Counsellors, Trainers, Counselling Skills and Supervision of Counsellors. In recent years, all those connected with helping and counselling have had their awareness of ethical issues raised by organisations such as BAC.

The BAC code of Ethics and Practice for Counsellors suggests that as counsellors we have responsibilities towards the client, ourselves as counsellors, colleagues and members of the caring professions and the wider community.

If you have not yet seen any of the above Codes, do obtain those that relate to your area of helping. They only cost a few pence each and are available from BAC at 1 Regent Place, Rugby, CV21 2PJ.

Supervision

You need to consider the following '*Four C's*' of ethical research before proceeding and if you have any doubts or uncertainties about any of them seek *supervision*. Yes, researchers have supervisors too! A research supervisor will be someone with more experience than you and may have a proven track-record in published research. Such people with a track-record in counselling or psychotherapy research may be difficult to find, so in the absence of a Counselling specialist, you could try the Social Science, Psychology or Sociology departments of your local University or College. If you are a student on a counselling course your lecturer may be able to help, or refer you to someone who can. You will need a minimum of a couple of meetings, one to outline your ideas and have them vetted and another to hear how you got on, look at your results to make sure you're treating them appropriately and check the sense behind your conclusions.

The 'Four C's' of Ethical Research
Competence

• You must work within your own limits. If you are unsure seek supervision. Seeking 'advice' is not enough since research is ongoing and has ongoing consequences. You will, therefore, need an ongoing relationship to plan your data collection and research.

This is research supervision. If you are a student you should at the very least, consult with your lecturer before proceeding.
• When conducting your study, do not claim to be more skilled or qualified than you really are. The general public are often very impressed by 'researchers'. Do not abuse this. If you are a student, say this from the outset.

Consent
• Always obtain the informed consent of the participants making sure that they fully understand what they are agreeing to, i.e. who you are, what the purpose of the study is, who (if anyone) is funding the study, what levels of confidentiality will be guaranteed.
• It is unethical to deceive people. You should emphasise sensitive aspects of the study, not cover them up. If, after supervision, you conclude that the research cannot be carried out without some deception, ask yourself if the study is really worth it.
• In all cases, participants should be debriefed afterwards so that they know what the study was about. You should be prepared to answer all questions they may ask. Participants own result should be made available to them. If this might cause distress you should not proceed. Seek supervision if the feedback at the end of a study is likely to cause distress.
• You must let participants withdraw from your study at any time (make sure they know this). You should be on the alert for any distress caused to participants and be ready to stop immediately, however inconvenient this may be to you. Remember that as a researcher, you will be in a position of influence. Do not abuse this position of power.
• If participants are not in a position to give their informed consent (possibly children, some people with psychotic illness or those with special needs), you should take special advice. In the case of children you will need the consent of the child's parent or guardian and a responsible person may need to be present or close by whilst you are conducting your study, e.g. school teacher. In the midst of all of these 'responsible' adults, don't forget to ask the child themselves.

• If you are carrying out a naturalistic observation of, for example, behaviour in public, you will not need the consent of those involved. You must, however, remember two things:
    i) Many 'public' places are in fact private properties (shopping precincts and airports) so ask permission first. (This includes permission to conduct surveys.) I remember some ill-prepared psychology students armed with camera and clipboard being carted off by security guards at Manchester Airport!
    ii) Be discreet and respect the privacy of the people you are observing. You will not want to end up with a black eye.

Confidentiality
This should not be a novel concept to helpers and counsellors.
- Treat all data as confidential.
- The participants in your study should not be able to be identified.
- Keep your records safe, so that others cannot gain access to them.

Conduct
- Always be honest about your own competence and limitations. Do not claim to be an expert in something that you are not. Put the welfare and safety of your participants first. Do not ask participants to do anything illegal. Do not put your participants at any risk at any time. Be prepared to abandon your study.

"You should never:
- insult, offend or anger participants
- make participants believe they have harmed or upset someone else
- break the law or encourage others to do so
- contravene the Data Protection Act
- illegally copy tests and materials
- make up data
- copy other people's work
- claim that someone else's wording is your own."
    p.5 Davies, Haworth and Hirschler, 'Ethics in Psychological Research' (ATP) 1992

In conclusion and as a final reminder, if you have any doubts about any of these areas you should seek supervision before you proceed. Unethical research is worse than useless; it has harmed either people or the reputation of counselling along the way. You must always start off by asking yourself, "Should I be conducting this kind of study at all?" to be sure you can justify your study to both yourself and anyone else who may ask you.

4 Qualitative Data Collection

It would be comforting to find a logical order in which to introduce the next topics - Qualitative Data Collection and Qualitative Data Analysis. However, the proverbial chicken and egg come to haunt us again since it's difficult to work out which comes first, data collection or data analysis. In the real world of research, data collection and analysis come in almost every possible order - it is possible to pre-determine your analysis by devising questionnaires or observation coding schemes with built-in categories, or you can leave the data analysis until after you've collected in all your data.

One point that researchers, both qualitative and quantitative, have agreed on over the years, is that you must have your methods of data analysis in mind when you start out collecting your data. This is good advice at all levels of research since you could spend many days, weeks, months and in some cases years collecting data which turns out to be un-analysable in terms of your research question because of some feature of your collection method. In other words you've got the wrong data for your chosen method of analysis or you've got the wrong method of analysis lined up for the data you've collected.

So, in order to avoid problems, we've got to keep in mind the realities of research which tell us that knowing about data collection is not enough preparation to go out and start collecting. You've got to know about data analysis before you start your research. You must read both the current chapter and the next one before you can start collecting your data.

What is data?

This may seem like a naive question to some readers, but like so many questions, the process of asking it and trying to answer it is just as important as the answers we might come up with. In the Compare and Contrast at the end of Chapter 1, the three examples gave very different ideas about what data could or should be. We could try to list all the possible categories of data which would be admissible to a research project, but since qualitative methods have broadened our expectations beyond measuring things with mere numbers, it is only our imagination that limits our research. Literally anything can be considered data for qualitative study from words in diaries and journals, through pictures and drawings to intuitions and feelings. We are no longer constrained by the idea that we have to be able to get a reliable measure of a particular variable.

That does not mean however, that we do not carefully, and diligently collect our data, and rigorously subject our data to some form of treatment, in order to discover and understand what information it may yield. It is important to remember that data collection and analysis are both mindful and, in their own way in qualitative approaches, disciplined activities. We must also keep in mind the methods of analysis we intend to use as we begin to plan how we will collect the data in the first place. A laissez-faire approach to research will nearly always end in an inconclusive jumble of information from which little can be learned. (This is in contrast to an inconclusive jumble of information which can be marshalled into some shape from which we can learn.)

The current chapter concerns methods of data collection in qualitative research. We intend it to be a comprehensive set of categories of data collection methods, whilst acknowledging that it isn't a comprehensive list of individual methods. Researchers have (so far) identified a limited (and some would say finite) number of possible ways of collecting data from the sources available. This chapter seeks to explain each of these possible ways and give some further detail of the creative methods employed by researchers in recent years. You will have to develop each general method yourself so that it and you together create, a unique data collection tool to suit your unique purpose. Creating your own tools is at the heart of qualitative research.

Certain themes are pursued in qualitative research. These themes spring from elements of the debate outlined in Chapter 1. As we proceed to describe and explain each method of data collection and analysis, it may help your understanding if you can keep these themes in mind.

Participation
Since qualitative researchers are interested in the effects that the researcher has on the situation being studied, and that they take the view that the best standpoint from which to develop an understanding is to see the world from the context within which the actors live, it stands to reason that participation is essential. Subjectivity is preferred to objectivity. Qualitative methodologists take the view that any observation interferes with the actions being observed anyway, so you might as well get right in the middle of it.

Action
Ideas associated with action research were first developed by Kurt Lewin in the 1940s, suggesting that social science research should be applied to practical everyday issues in the real world. The basic method is to enter a social setting, try to change it in some way and monitor the results. Trying to influence the sexual behaviour of young adults since the discovery AIDS would be an example of action research.

Collaboration
People participating in research programmes in the traditional paradigm are called *subjects*. This gives some idea of the role of the subject as being someone with little power, someone *subjected*

to the experimental treatments etc. Subjects are not asked for their views and historically have even been deceived as to the true purpose of the research. In qualitative approaches, we seek collaboration with our participants. They can be called actors, participants, people or whatever but never *subjects*. We will fully inform them of the purpose of the study, involve them in planning the work, ask about their thoughts and feelings during the research, even ask them to help in the data analysis.

Repetition
One of the key ideas in quantitative research is that your results should be reliable. That is to say that your results should be consistent from one time to the next. This concept fails to acknowledge actively, and exploit the notion that human beings, their actions and meanings, are far from consistent and that this may, in itself, be both interesting and worthy of study. Notwithstanding the inherent inconsistency of humans, qualitative researchers also pursue a type of reliability. This they try to achieve primarily by repeating the research cycle. If anything changes it is worth noting and paying attention to, just as it is if nothing changes.

Contextualisation
It is central to our understanding of the validity of any research finding in qualitative work, that we understand the context of the action we are studying. The human-beingness that we are interested in is viewed organically and holistically, and without a context it becomes meaningless. As holistic researchers we would no more conduct a study on friendship in a laboratory than try to understand what the human heart does by taking it out of a living body.

In fact, qualitative work goes further than this. It could be said that the understanding of a piece of human dynamics lies in the context itself and without the context the action doesn't exist. So finding and understanding the context of human action is the very essence of qualitative work. The interesting issue lies in how flexible we are in our definitions of the idea of 'context'.

Chapter 4 Overview
Qualitative Data Collection

I Observing others and ourselves 68
Participant observation, 69
Self observation, 72
Role play and simulation, 74
Human inquiry groups, 76
How to collect and record your observations 77

II Interrogating others and exploring their experience 88
Some answers about questions, 89
Questionnaires, 93
Interviews, 98

III Looking at what's left behind 108
Documents and records, 109
Published media, 109
Broadcast media, 109
Physical traces, 109

IV Other Methods 111
Repertory Grid techniques, 111
Interpersonal Process Recall, 113
Meta Analysis, 114
Q-Methodology, 115
Action research, 115

I Observing others and ourselves

Participant observation

One of the first ways of collecting data that occurs to anyone interested in researching human actions and their meaning is to watch what people do, make some kind of record of the observations then describe and possibly analyse the observed actions. There are several variations of the method of observation which can be placed somewhere along a continuum depending upon whether the observer participates in the action or not.

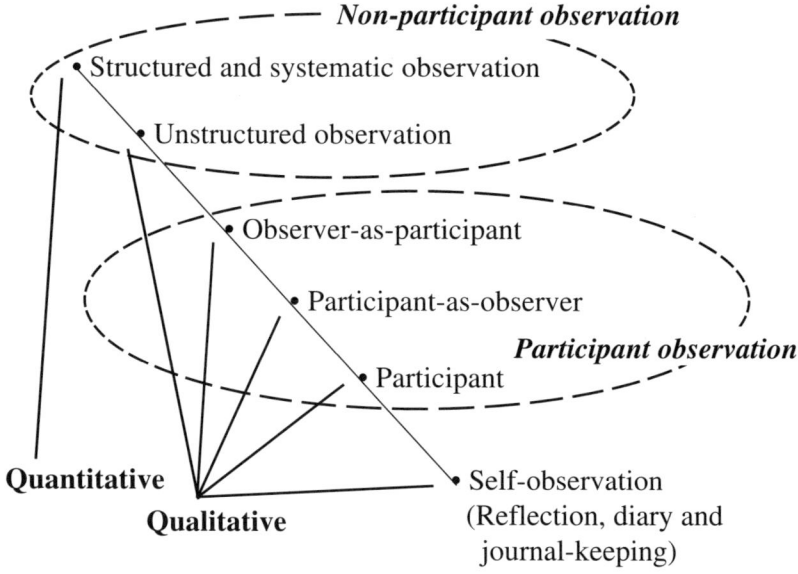

At the one extreme is the systematic, structured observation where the observer is not connected with the action at all, sometimes separated from the action by glass (one-way mirror), or time and place (video tape). This is a quantitative method because firstly it seeks to remove the observer and their effects from the action being observed. Secondly the observer observes in a pre-determined highly structured and systematic way, using various numerical coding methods with which to capture the behaviour. So, the observer is removed from the action in order to promote the objectivity and neutrality of the observations and the actions being observed are counted according to a scheme pre-determined by the researcher. We will look at the other, qualitative types of observation in more detail.

Qualitative non-participant observation
It is possible to observe and record the actions of others in an initially unquantified, descriptive form. This method involves unstructured observation where the observer describes what is observed rather than categorising or interpreting and counting actions. In all cases of qualitative observation, including those that follow, the term 'actions' can refer to any or all behaviour in whatever natural and complex form including language and interactions with others.

This method of observation was pioneered in psychology by *ethologists* such as Lorenz and Tinbergen from the 1940s onwards. Ethology is the study of animal behaviour in natural settings. Whilst some ethologists prefer to set out mini experiments in the field, others notably Tinbergen would spend hours watching or recording animals on film then painstakingly describing what the animals did. From the patterns of movement, the ethologists would seek an understanding of, for example, territorial or courtship behaviour.

An ethological approach can be taken with human beings and their actions, but most studies following an unstructured observational method resort to counting behaviour eventually.

Example: Robinson and Whitfield (1987) made audio tape recordings of consultations between trainee general practitioners and their patients with the consent of the participants. These recordings were then subjected to analysis which showed that the involvement of the patients in the consultation depended upon the communication skills of the doctor. As counsellors we might find this hardly surprising.

Advantages: Since the observer is removed from the action and hopes to interfere with it as little as possible, film, video and audio tape recorders can be used. Data collection can be streamlined.

Disadvantages: The flipside of the advantages to streamlined data collection can leave you with quantitative data or data that has lost any human touch. The method also generates huge amounts of data such as voluminous transcripts of audio tapes, or page upon page of the observer's frantic shorthand notes.

Observer-as-participant
This and the following two types of observation are distinguished by the degree to which the observer takes part in the action and the degree to which their role as observer is known by the other actors. The observer-as-participant is a person who is separate from the action in that they take no part in it, but their role as researcher is known to the actors. It is a type of conscious journalistic approach to observation in which the observer reports on the action from the privileged position of researcher without having to get involved.

Example: This method has been favoured by traditional anthropologists who would place themselves in the midst of another culture and describe what they saw. Margaret Mead (1928) brought this approach to the attention of the world in her book *Coming of Age in Samoa,* in which she describes an observational study of young women in Samoa. She used a variety of structured and descriptive methods over a period of nine months during which Mead lived amongst the people she was observing.

Advantages: Not as demanding as more involving or participatory styles of observation. Pre-determined coding can be used, making the method lean more towards quantitative methods.

Disadvantages: It is debatable that anyone can reveal themselves to be an observer or researcher in the midst of the action without at some level becoming a part of the action and influencing it in some way. It is dangerous to assume that the observer has little or no effect. The effect of the observer will always be a central part of the action. This method makes it difficult to manage data collection.

Participant-as-observer
In this type of observation the observer might declare their role as observer at the start of the action being observed and then seek to establish relationships with other actors as if s/he were one of them. Alternatively, the observer role is seen as not the main reason for the participant's presence, but as an adjunct to their already existing role, e.g. you may decide to observe relationships at your workplace. This is a difficult role to fill as it puts strain on the observer being in two roles. It also stands a great chance of disturbing or influencing the action as it develops.

Example: Maruyama (1981) reported on a project where prisoners constituted the research team to study various aspects of prison culture. The report includes a detailed description of the team's struggles to become a cohesive research unit and interesting accounts of the role conflict experienced by the researchers themselves.

Advantages: This method can be a convenient way to observe the action of which you are already a part. It holds the promise of not being too disruptive to any action that is already in progress.

Disadvantages: Can cause role-tension and be subject to more observer effects (see p.78) than other forms of participant observation. Needs careful preparation.

Full participant
Here the observer becomes an actor in the action without ever revealing their role as observer. The true purpose of their presence in the group is concealed from the other actors.

Example: An early and seminal example of this kind of research was described by Festinger et al (1956) where he and his accomplices infiltrated a religious group who believed that the world was going to end on a particular day. Festinger joined the group and recorded their actions as they waited for the end to come, and their reactions and explanations when the predictions turned out to be false.

Advantages: This method suggests that it might get as close to 'real life' as possible by locating the observer incognito in the thick of the action. The aim is to be unobtrusive (indeed undiscovered) and therefore, so the argument goes, un*intrusive* as far as the recorded actions go.

Disadvantages: As with other methods requiring an element of deception, this raises ethical issues regarding informed consent of the participants. Also, following on from the advantages above, it is argued that even this method is not truly unobtrusive, since the presence of the observer is by definition an artefact. It could never be known what might have happened had the observer not been present. To extrapolate this idea, it might even be the case that researchers behave in a way that distorts the action through more active collusion with, or manipulation of, the actors to achieve a desired result. Such behaviour is clearly unethical.

Self-observation

Recording one's own experiences is not simply a component of other qualitative methods such as participant observation, but also an activity that may run in parallel to it to enhance or illuminate the descriptions of other actors behaviour. It is also a complete and valid qualitative research method in its own right. If you are not intimidated by other people's visions of what data is or can be, you can be creative in terms of the media used to record and represent your experiences. Self observation can be the backbone of a single case study (see p.28) covering a discrete event or sequence of events in your life.

• *Self-observation as a component of participant observation*: In this case the observer may have a category of observation reserved for their own actions as part of the overall action. It is inevitable

that in some participant-observer studies, the observer themselves will become such a central part of the action that their own behaviour must be recorded.
• *Self-observation as a complimentary parallel process*: Keeping a journal or diary is a favourite method of logging one's own thoughts, feeling, and actions, and their personal meanings. If kept at the same time as the observations are made, such a personal record is useful when the main observational data is scrutinised. The observer's part in the action, hitherto hidden, may become revealed as the emotional life of the observer and actors are seen alongside each other.
• *Self-observation as a research activity in its own right*: The method of *introspection* was developed over 100 years ago by the German psychologist Wilhelm Wundt. Although Wundt's introspection was a highly disciplined, restrictive method of self-sensing and awareness development, it serves to emphasise that anyone hoping to engage in any serious self-observation must prepare themselves thoroughly. Self-observation can become a rambling, self-centred diatribe serving little purpose. Along with all other observation methods this requires some discipline and not a little rigour.

Techniques:
Memo writing: Involves writing memos to yourself, helping you develop your thoughts by writing them down as they occur. The ideas and thoughts don't have to be at any stage of completion, or even make 'sense'. One function of memo writing is to unburden your mind so that you are free to observe the action of others or free to have more ideas. A memo to yourself is also one way of trapping ideas, intuitions and interpretations before they are forgotten.
Diaries: Most readers will be familiar with the notion of keeping diaries. The distinction between diaries and journals is that diaries are usually thought to be more personal and reflective in nature. Diaries can tell the 'feeling story' behind the action, giving insight into your inner world of meanings which may be missing from more dry observations.

Journals and logs: Journals and field logs are a record of what happened to you and when. They are narrative and descriptive accounts of the period under study with dates, times and places as required. Some of these elements may be missing from the more haphazard and personal accounts in diaries.

Examples: Several examples of different approaches to self-observation can be found in Reason and Rowan (1981), two of which can be summarised as follows:
Collin (1981) adopts a self-reflective style to look at how developing as a researcher through her research changes her career aspirations and personal requirements.
Reason (1981) gives an account of how the 'subjects' themselves became the 'researchers' into interpersonal dynamics within couples by participating in workshops.

Advantages: Gives the essential researcher's perspective, important in all qualitative research but necessary when the researcher is so self-consciously a part of the action being studied. Gives invaluable supporting evidence to other data. Counsellors might find themselves drawn to the experiential nature of this type of research. Allows others access to unique experiences through novel and exciting media.

Disadvantages: Requires discipline and attention that few people can muster without much preparation or training. Can be tedious to perform - a feeling which must, of course, be noted in your diary! Can become a licence for self-indulgent accounts of our lives.

Role play and simulation

These have been used extensively in social psychology research and attracted considerable controversy. These methods are usually 'laboratory observation' where the observers are removed from the action and where the participants or actors in the role play do not know the true purpose of the study or, most contentiously of all, where the actors do not even know that it is a simulation or role-play.

Examples: Famous studies on obedience (Milgram 1963) and bystander apathy (Piliavin et al 1969)) demonstrate the technique and highlight the ethical issues that arise.

Milgram (1963) reported a study in which members of the public answered an advert to take part in a psychological study of memory. They did not know that the true purpose of the study was to look at obedience to instructions. They were asked to act as 'teacher' to another person as 'learner' who had also answered the same advert. (Little did they know that the 'learner' was an accomplice of the experimenter.) They were asked to administer electric shocks of increasing severity to the learner whenever the learner got a task wrong, eventually administering a 'fatal' shock. Some subjects were led to believe that they had killed another volunteer in the name of 'science'.

Piliavin et al (1969) set up a situation in the 'real world' in which an accomplice would 'collapse' in the carriage whilst travelling on the New York subway. Sometimes the accomplice seemed ill, sometimes they smelled of drink. They observed and recorded the behaviour of witnesses and passers-by.

Other studies demonstrate at least the informed consent and increasingly active collaboration with participants. Miller and Brown (1985) for example, report on one simulation called the 'Mini Economy' lasting three days in which participants (including the observers) lived out the consequences of replicating the economic forces of society in a microcosm. Participants collaborated with the initial setting up of the project and were subsequently involved in data processing. (Reported more fully in Miller 1993)

Advantages: Role plays and simulations allow some control over the situation whilst leaving the actors free to 'be themselves' as much as is possible. The time, place and other factors can be pre-determined for convenience of the observer(s) and actors. Collaboration and consultation is not only possible but desirable, including feedback after the event. If you follow properly ethical procedures the actors will know that the scenario is a role-play and simulation and may be invited to keep their own accounts as diaries or journals and they will have the opportunity to habituate to any cameras or microphones present.

Disadvantages: Often these are the flip-sides of the advantages. Staged scenarios like this often never lose that artificial quality and so will affect the nature of the action (the degree to which this affects the actors can be checked). Some simulations in social psychology have 'gone wrong' and had to be terminated, e.g. the infamous prisoner-guard simulation reported by Haney, Banks and Zimbardo (1970) in which the 'guards' became too involved and ended up physically assaulting the 'prisoners'. Even if such drastic consequences are avoided, participants must be carefully selected and briefed, then fully debriefed afterwards and offered support if necessary.

Human Inquiry Groups

Not to be confused with the *simulations* of the type described by Miller (1993), human inquiry groups have developed from the work of Reason and Rowan (1981). A human inquiry group is a group set up with the dual purposes of helping the members develop their awareness and understanding of the issue at hand (this may be a common theme in their lives, like survival of a disaster, or having a near-death experience), whilst at the same time researching the 'topic' in a highly collaborative, participant-observation style.

Example: There are only a few examples of this person-as-participant-as-researcher method, since it is a recent development from the ideas introduced by Reason and Rowan (1981). Reason (1981) describes a group experience whereby couples learned about interpersonal communication whilst researching their own communications within the couples. You can, of course, say it the other way round (they researched interpersonal communication in couples whilst in a group focusing upon raising awareness of interpersonal communication in those couples) to demonstrate the inter-dependence of the 'group experience' and the 'research' elements.

Miller and Brown (1985) report a Social Economy Research Group (SERG) at a 4-day conference in 1985 in which self-selected participants were recording their own conference interpersonal behaviour and processing it at group meetings throughout the conference. A participant's view of the experience is reported by Sanders (1986).

Advantages: A very 'grounded' style of qualitative study. Has strong 'action' and collaborative themes. Could be very useful for counselling/therapy applications where an empathic/developmental approach is required.

Disadvantages: Very demanding of time and effort. Requires self-observation and report skills in all participants (can be developed as part of the experience). Preparation required.

How to collect and record your observations.
Installing yourself as an observer

The first task facing observers is to gain reasonable ethical access to the action being observed. This can be more involved than you might initially think. Participant observation hinges upon a number of factors including observer preparation (see page 58) and the quality of the relationship between the observer and the other actors. Many of the examples give above required many days, weeks or months during which the observers got to know the other actors and to varying extents became members of the groups they were observing. In some cases where the observer's role was kept secret, this may have involved a period of induction into the group and the gaining of their trust.

As counsellors you will be familiar with, and hopefully competent in, the skills of relationship-building. Entering a group as a participant observer is no more or less complicated than building relationships at the start of counselling either in groups or with individuals. The key qualities are genuineness (particularly *being yourself*), being non-judgemental (being judgemental is no more the role of the researcher than it is the role of the counsellor), and empathy (essential if your observations are to be worthwhile).

Observer effects
These are the consequences of participant observation, i.e. how the actions of those being observed change as a result of being observed.
- It is never possible to be completely sure that the presence of an observer has no effect.
  There are some signs to look out for that the observer is successfully integrated into the group:
  Other actors show less and less interest in the observer, including making less contact which acknowledges the role of observer.
  Other actors say that the presence of the observer is having little or no effect. This can be checked with other participants, e.g. doctors may say that nothing has changed as a consequence of the observation, but patients may say that the doctors spend more time with each patient.
  Observations stabilise after an initial period.
- Some researchers believe that it is important to acknowledge the inevitability of observer effects and incorporate them into the data collection.
  This can be done through deliberate collaboration and consultation with the participants.

Collecting and recording data
When you have decided how you will successfully install yourself as an observer you have to decide how you are going to collect your data and what methods you will use to record it. There are several recording methods to choose from some helped by new technology, then the recorded material (raw data) needs to be treated or possibly refined in some way in order to reveal the meanings hidden in it. This is called *coding*. The accuracy and usefulness of coding depends to a large extent on how transparent or unbiased the coding instrument is and since the coding instrument in qualitative research is the researcher themselves, or their appointed helper, we will look at some ways of dealing with observational

biases. Of course, in qualitative research this will occasionally mean not trying to eliminate bias but rather incorporating the effect and meaning such biases into our study in a mindful way.

Sometimes recording observations and coding can be carried out simultaneously in the same operation. This is when the observation system is based on pre-determined checklists or category systems where the observer ticks boxes at the time of observation. This is a more structured method leaning more than a little in the direction of quantitative methods. Whilst there is always an element of pre-planning in all research, we will not be dealing here with treatment and coding schemes which are heavily structured and pre-determined. We will limit our attention to fairly lightweight coding at the time of observation as an aid to the observer. Coding observations after the event will be dealt with in Chapter 5 on Data Treatment, p.122.

We would find it almost impossible to collect any data if we were simply instructed to 'Observe and record the important bits of the following counselling session'. What are we expected to observe? How do we know what is important? We go into each observation period with some pre-determined plan as to how we are going to look at the action in question and which bits we are going to record. There is a wide range of possibilities when it comes to recording and coding human actions, each of which we will have decided before we start. The following scale uses examples which only serve to illustrate the qualitative - quantitative, structured - unstructured continua on which observational studies can be placed. Each 'example' looks at *observation - recording - coding - data treatment.* **Note:** *The first phase of any observation study will be largely exploratory. After the exploratory phase the researcher will then determine what features the study will have:*
- *To what extent the observation will be structured and pre-determined.*
- *To what extent the observations will be coded on-site.*
- *How much the observer will record of their own behaviour.*

• *What treatment of the data will take place once it is all collected in.*

The scale has four positions on it to illustrate the degrees of structure possible relating to the points above:

1
Observe as much as possible - record everything, including your own thoughts, feelings and actions, and any collaboration with participants - code nothing at the time of observation - sort and categorise later when all the data is in.
This is at the extreme qualitative end of the questionnaire spectrum. It requires a lot of time and patience both to build up relationships with other actors in order for the observations to stabilise and to make the actual observations. All data treatment is done after the event using qualitative methods (see pp.117-137) since the recording of the observations is done in a 'freehand' style with no pre-determined coding scheme.

2
Observe as much as possible - record a large sample of the action, record your own feelings, thought and actions - use a loose general coding scheme to categorise the action at the time, consider your self-related data later - further sort and categorise your observations when all the data is in.
A largely qualitative approach with some features of quantitative methods to manage the amount of data coming in by sampling plus possibly coding the data in situ with a view to some small quantitative analysis for triangulation purposes. The person of the researcher is still very much at the heart of the data collection and analysis.

3
Observe a restricted portion of the action - record only some of it, possibly keeping a separate diary of your thoughts and feelings e.g. whether you were tired and fatigued - use a structured coding scheme to categorise the data at the time of observation, possibly use your diary if it adds to the data

significantly, (do not consult participants) - some limited further sorting and categorising to do when all the data is in. Leaning more towards quantitative than qualitative methodology, here the observer takes a more fringe position but is nevertheless involved in the study more than in quantitative non-participant observation. Coding is both pre-determined to a large extent and geared towards numerical quantification of behaviour, but there is still room for the subjective impressions of the observer to add that qualitative edge in support of the findings.

4

Observe a small, finite portion of the action - record only that which falls into your coding scheme ignore the rest - use a tightly structured coding scheme to categorise data at the time of observation, don't record your own thoughts or feelings, or consult participants - no need for further data treatment when all the data is in other than statistical analysis.
This is structured quantitative observation. We will not be looking at this in any detail in this book.

Recording your observations
There are many methods for recording behaviour. Firstly you need to decide what sampling method you are going to use. That is to say, are you going to try to record all behaviour, or just a portion of it determined by, for example time or location? Then you must decide which method of recording is most appropriate.

Sampling
Two decisions need to be made in sampling, firstly what proportion of the action is to be recorded and secondly, what will determine the onset and offset of the recording.
• Time sampling is when a time interval, pre-determined according to some pattern (which may be random) is used to observe behaviour. E.g. if a two hour group supervision is being observed, it could be decided to record the whole session, or to record ten, five minute periods at random over the whole two hour session.

- Location sampling is when only action occurring at a specific location is recorded. E.g. nurses' behaviour whilst at the patients' bedsides.
- Event sampling is when you record all behaviour following or associated with a particular event, e.g. recording all counsellor or client responses after silences of ten seconds or more.

Recording

However unstructured the observation method is, a careful and systematic recording of observations is essential.

General features of a recording:
Spradley (1980) identified the following dimensions for the collection of data in observations:
- Description of the physical space, e.g. diagrams of layout.
- Other physical features and objects such as furniture.
- Names and relevant other information about the actors.
- The actions of the actors.
- Specific events and occasions such as formal or informal meetings.
- The timed sequence of events.
- Information about what the actors were trying to achieve in the way of aims.
- Feelings and emotions of actors.

We might add to this list some dimensions concerning the observer in participant observation:
- How the observer is feeling before during and after the observation session.
- Why the observer participated in the action.
- Any intuitions or interpretations occurring at the time of observation.

Written records:
- Ideally, a record should be made on the spot, as it happens. You may need to develop a system of shorthand or abbreviations.

- When each observation session is finished, the abbreviated record should be augmented with detail and expanded accounts of the action. Lofland and Lofland (1984) suggest the following contents of a well-documented record:
  - *Running descriptions* - specific descriptions of observed events without the observer's inferences or interpretations.
  - *Recall of forgotten material* - bits and pieces of the action that you remember later.
  - *Interpretive ideas* - the observers interpretations, analysis, possible explanations and inferences. These can be focused on the research question or tangential to it.
  - *Personal impressions and feelings* - the observer's subjective reactions either at the time or subsequent to the observation.
  - *Reminders* - notes to attend to in the next session, perhaps to look out for a certain event, sequence or connection of events.
- Add as much as is necessary so that you will be able to 're-create' the action on subsequent reading of the record. Don't put this off - time will degrade your memory of events and after a few sessions you will start confusing one session with another, as well as the order in which events happened.

Film, video or audio tape records:
Frequently used in non-participant observation, these automated recording devices can also be useful to augment participant observation.
- It is always worth checking that you can operate the equipment and that it is working properly before the beginning of each session.
- Always make sure that the other actors know that they are being recorded (see Chapter 3 p.57 on ethics).
- Automatic recording media cannot record the observer's subjective thoughts and feelings. You will have to do this later. Make any such records as soon as possible after the

session, your memory will only fade.
• Another obvious point that regularly gets overlooked - label all recordings with the time, date and place as minimum. Keep the recordings safe - for your sake and to protect what might be confidential information.
• As soon as possible after the recording is made and always before the next one is made view or listen to the recording to check the quality. Attend to any technical problems that arise.
• Attach to each recording any special note - things to look out for or be aware of when watching or subsequently coding the record.
• Make a separate recordings log - date, time, duration, place, name of participant observer(s), media and recording equipment used and any reminders for the next session regarding camera position, sound levels etc.

Note: *Be judicious in you use of such recording methods. They generate a huge quantity of data which will take a very long time to code. Make sure you have the time and resources to analyse it in the way you want to. The flip-side of this is that such records are very durable and can always be returned to at a later date, indeed you may wish to do this anyway as a planned repetition of your research cycle.*

Pre determined coding schemes
The development of a coding scheme is difficult and time consuming. The following steps are involved, each one requiring some consideration and exploratory data collection (called piloting) to test it out before you go ahead and use it in your study proper:

1. How many observers are you going to use?
   If there is more that one you will have to train each observer to observe in a standard way using the coding scheme you have developed.
2. Are the observations global or specific?
   When we create a coding scheme for global observations, we usually call this a rating scale. Counsellors may be

familiar with the work of Truax and Carkhuff in their rating of Rogers' core conditions. Specific observations are dealt with depending upon the number and type of categories of event being observed.
3. How many types of event do you want to observe?
   If a small number of events are to be observed, it may be possible to construct a scheme which records some detail about each event in terms of sub-categories. A large number of categories of event will limit your coding scheme to a checklist. You may have broad general categories each with a checklist, e.g. Non-verbal behaviours (plus checklist), Spatial behaviours (plus checklist), Extra-linguistic behaviours (plus checklist) and Linguistic behaviours (plus checklist).
4. What use will your categories really be?
   Don't fall into the trap of trying to record everything just because you can see it. If absolutely necessary have a catch-all 'other' category to dump interesting bits into, rather than leave them out. Tie your coding to your hypothesis or research question as tightly as possible.
5. How objective do you want it to be?
   It pays to be explicit about any inferences or interpretations you expect your observer(s) to make. Even if you are the sole observer, you need to be clear where on the subjectivity-objectivity scale you are. Using a pre-determined coding scheme is more than a nod in the direction of objectivity and quantification, so try not to mix models.
6. Make your categories mutually exclusive.
   Do not have any overlapping categories. They should be independent which means one category for each separate thing.
7. Make life easy for your observer(s).
   Especially if you are the sole observer! If you are leaning towards quantitative analysis make the system user-friendly, e.g. tick-boxes where possible, simple abbreviations and explicitly defined categories which leave little or no room for error. If you are inclined towards a more qualitative approach be sure that you really want a pre-determined coding scheme in the first place, then make your categories

global with plenty of room for subjective opinion.
8. Don't re-invent the wheel.
There are several good examples of coding schemes for human behaviour in the literature. You may decide to use one 'off the peg'. Counsellors may already be familiar with Bales' Interaction Categories or Heron's Six Category Intervention Analysis.

Bias in observation due to human factors
Every observer brings their unique personality to the task of observation and imposes themselves upon the process of observation and hence the results. In quantitative research we would seek to remove this observer bias by strict controls to expunge the effects of the observer from the results. Qualitative observation, however, embraces the observer and their biases through participation and collaboration.

We mentioned in Chapter 3 that the human instrument needs regular 'servicing' and 'calibration' if it is to be of any use in qualitative studies. However much we prepare ourselves for observation there are certain built in tendencies in the ways humans work which we simply must accept. We should be aware of and try to understand these human qualities as we proceed to plan our qualitative observational study. We can then choose to incorporate, ignore or exclude these human factors as appropriate to our research design.

Readers with a background in psychology will be aware of these areas of bias in human functioning - the following is just a reminder to watch out for the human factor! If you wish to know more and do not have a background in psychology we recommend *Psychology -Theory and Application* by Banyard and Hayes (1994):

Attention - Our past experiences and expectations of the future shape our ability to pay attention to the world. Psychologists call it *selective attention* to emphasise that human beings have a limited capacity to attend to varied and complex information. The fact that humans pay attention selectively means that we are more likely to turn our attention to those parts of the environment that we think hold the most important information. (See Banyard and Hayes pp 348-55.) In qualitative methodology we should be aware of this feature of human attention so that we can understand the nature of human subjectivity.

Another feature of our ability to pay attention to things is *attenuation*, that is to say the fact that we get used to a particular event to such an extent that we fail to see it any more. As an observer, it is crucial that we do not attenuate to the events we are observing.

Perception - Our perception of other persons and objects in the environment is subject to many influences including our past experiences and development, the things we last looked at, what we expect to be looking at, etc. The factors that influence the sense we make of the world are certainly too numerous to mention here. One very strong factor which predisposes us to see and hear certain things and not others is called *perceptual set*. It means that we expect to see certain patterns of events and sometimes distort the world so that we see what we expect rather than what is there. (See Banyard and Hayes pp 350-60.)

Our perception of people is no more reliable and as counsellors we have a keen appreciation of this. A plethora of psychological effects confronts us in the realm of interpersonal perception and communication. If you are interested or feel you need to understand some of the issues further read Banyard and Hayes pp 123-83 and 341-48.

Memory - We don't need psychologists to tell us that our memory plays tricks on us! However, we might be surprised to learn just how human memory is flawed. One example is that we tend to remember the first and last things that happen in a sequence much better than those things in the middle of the sequence. This is called primacy and recency effect and has obvious implications for observation studies. (See Banyard and Hayes pp 348-55.)

II Interrogating others and exploring their experience

This sub-title refers to ways of finding out about other people's lives and experiences by using *questionnaires* and *interviews*. Both questionnaires and interviews can be more-or-less structured. Structured approaches use various types of questions either on paper or spoken - this we call *interrogation*. Unstructured approaches do not use questions, but facilitate the respondent's telling of their story by reflective techniques - this we call *exploration*. Many researchers do not hold a firm position at the extremes of this dimension of relative structure, they use a mixture of techniques to capture a broad range of experiences from their respondents. Others prefer a structured approach because they lean towards the apparent rigour of the quasi-quantitative feel of a pre-determined set of questions. Yet others espouse an unstructured, reflective approach because it seems more congruent with the human processes at the heart of qualitative inquiry.

As counsellors we will be familiar with the dilemma of structure in the exploration of the worlds of our clients. Some counsellors believe that the sensitive and judicious use of questions and probes helps the client's explore the issues they bring, whilst other counsellors prefer to not ask questions at all in the belief that it puts the counsellor and his/her agenda at the centre of the process and thus prevents the client from exploring their world in a way that will be purposeful, fulfilling and healing. This, then is the dilemma of research if you simply change a few of the words. The aim in research is not resolution or self-actualisation (although these can be exciting by-products of the research process!), rather the goal is the discovery of meaning that has the 'ring of truth' for the respondent, as free from the *unidentified, undisclosed* clutter of the researcher's agenda as possible. How do we achieve this?

Some answers about questions

Unless you are opting for the extreme of an unstructured, reflective, respondent-centred interview with no questions at all, you will have to spend some time thinking about the sort of questions you want to use. Questions are common to both questionnaires and interviews, so we will review the options regarding questions before we look at how questions might be marshalled into some form of interrogation device.

Closed and open questions: Counsellors will be familiar with the distinction between closed and open questions:

Closed questions
These offer a fixed number of alternative answers to choose from giving the respondent limited freedom. Some closed questions ask for a response on a scale of some sort, perhaps of agreement or disagreement, preference or strength of feelings.

E.g. Are you currently in therapy?

Do you see your therapist
- *Less than once per week?*
- *Once per week?*
- *Twice per week?*
- *More than twice per week?*

Do you find your therapist
- *1 Very effective?*
- *2 Effective?*
- *3 Neither effective nor ineffective?*
- *4 Ineffective?*
- *5 Very ineffective?*

Advantages: Structured interrogation uses mostly (if not all) closed questions. They can be useful for getting basic demographic information - name, age, or whatever else may be necessary to identify and help categorise your respondents. If you are trying to approximate a qualitative method, you must use closed questions very sparingly.

Disadvantages: Closed questions are the stock-in-trade of quantitative researchers, since they lend themselves to having numbers applied to their well-ordered and (if you've set and asked them correctly) predictable responses. They require careful phrasing since it is easy to ask a question which does not give the full range of answers for a particular group of respondents (you will only get the answers you provide). This makes closed questions unpopular with qualitative researchers because they impose the researcher's agenda upon the respondent.

Open Questions

Well known as a technique from the tool-kit of many counselling approaches, the open question does not give an answer or range of possible answers. It structures the interrogation only to the point of introducing the researcher's preferred agenda topic, but after that it does not direct the respondent to a set of permitted answers. The respondent can answer a well compiled, open question in almost any way they choose - including giving a 'nonsense' answer or avoiding the question.

> E.g.
> • *Why did you decide to enter therapy?*
> • *What do you look for when choosing a therapist?*
> • *How would you describe the effectiveness of your current therapist?*

Advantages: Since fewer constraints are imposed on the respondent they are less likely to feel frustrated - a happy respondent is an honest and more accurate respondent. Open questions get richer responses. Answers are potentially more accurate and representative since the respondent can talk around the question and reveal any misunderstandings which may remain hidden in answers to closed questions.

Disadvantages: Open question are more difficult to code in the traditional quantitative sense - you can't really apply numbers to the answers with ease. Open questions do not really lend themselves to questionnaires since respondents may get fatigued quite quickly.

If respondents are writing their responses, it can be difficult to judge how much space to allow for an answer since people will assume they have to fill the space allowed.

Other interrogation techniques
Questions aren't the only method of eliciting information in interviews. Counsellors will know of a range of interview skills that all help the respondent to tell their story. In planning an interview we need to consider what methods other than questions we might need to use in order to oil the wheels of data collection:

Silence: Counsellors know the value of silence in therapeutic interviews. Remember that the interviewer remaining silent is one way of getting the respondent to talk!

Continuation responses: Again, well known to counsellors - the smiles, 'Uh-huh' and 'I see' type responses keep the respondent talking, so don't forget to use them.

Probes: Specific questions to get the respondent to elaborate on a particular point. Particularly useful in semi-structured interviews, e.g.

> *'What do you look for when choosing a therapist?'*
> **Probe**: Ask for more about gender and ethnic origin.

Prompts: A range or set of possible answers or set of reminders to let the respondent know of any options they might not have thought about. Again, useful in semi-structured interviews, e.g.

> *'What do you look for when choosing a therapist?'*
> **Prompt**: show list of professional organisations if membership of a professional body is mentioned.

Some principles of question-asking
Wherever they are to be used, questions need to be carefully complied, sensitively asked and their answers treated with respect.

Here are some general rules which will help make your question-asking effective and efficient:
- *Ask questions that can be understood* - ask questions using language content and structure appropriate for your respondents. Try and put *your* question into the words your *respondents* would use.
- *Ask questions that do not lead to an obvious answer* - 'leading' questions either suggest an answer, make an assumption or imply something about the respondent, e.g. 'Why do you like your counsellor?' is better asked as, 'Do you like your counsellor?' Similarly, 'What makes Gestalt therapy superior to all other approaches?' should be rephrased as, 'What approach do you think is the best?' or, 'Do you think there are any advantages to Gestalt therapy?'
- *Ask the simplest and shortest question possible* - avoid jargon words unless they will be familiar to your respondents. People may only answer part of multi-part or long-winded questions, or simply not understand the question because it is difficult to make sense of or see how it hangs together.
- *Ask only questions that* **can** *be answered* - 'When was the last time you had a headache?' or, 'How many clients did you see in 1989?' will be difficult for respondents to answer accurately depending upon certain factors (e.g. whether they had a headache recently or whether they keep good records).
- *Ask only questions that* **will** *be answered* - This includes the principle which says you should ask questions that will be answered truthfully. An untruthful answer is of little use since you will not be able to sort out the true responses from the untruthful ones. A refusal, although it will produce a 'hole' in your data, is often better. 'Do you enjoy oral sex?', or, 'Have you behaved unethically in the past year?' might get refused. Respondents also object to being forced by a structured question to give an answer that doesn't accurately represent their experience.
- *Ask as few questions as possible* - your time is precious, and respect your respondent's time too. You should collect only that data which you need for the purposes of your study.

- Make sure the questions are relevant. This will make your project streamlined, elegant, or in research terms, *parsimonious*.

Questionnaires

Most of us are familiar with questionnaires of one sort or another, whether they be *market research* questionnaires administered on the high street, or *quality improvement* questionnaires about the service at your car dealer's. A questionnaire is always an attempt to limit, direct and order the information coming from the respondent. In this sense they are always leaning towards quantitative methodology. So, although genuine questionnaires *can* be structured to a greater or lesser degree they are all structured and to some extent pre-determined.

Essentially a questionnaire is a list of questions and instructions which the respondent is expected to fill in or complete themselves in the absence of the researcher.

Questionnaires manage the data flow from the respondent by limiting and directing it according to the researcher's agenda. This makes the use of questionnaires almost a borderline qualitative/ quantitative method, but one that those interested in developing qualitative methods will use with caution after much consideration.

In this section we will look briefly at the types of less tightly structured questionnaire that may be developed for use in qualitative studies. We will also look at other forms of self-completion activities which are much less structured than questionnaires. We will assume that the respondent has to complete the activity in writing - any method requiring a verbal response in the presence of the researcher we have decided to call an interview, including the use of the telephone, (although we have not dealt with the telephone separately).

The setting of the questionnaire

By this we mean the circumstances the respondent will be receiving and completing the questionnaire. There is a range of settings from formal to informal:

- A room at the researcher's premises, on their own, with an

'invigilator' to help with problems and misunderstandings.
• As above in a group.
• At home, delivered by prior arrangement by the researcher. The researcher stays to introduce the questionnaire and give some instructions.
• At home by post, by prior arrangement.
• At home by post, without prior arrangement.
• As above but at the respondent's place of work.

Each setting will affect the level and quality of responses given by the respondents. The following factors should be considered:
• How many questionnaires are likely to be returned. (Postal questionnaires do not get a very high response rate - between 20 - 50%.)
• Distractions to the respondent during completion.
• Interrupted or non-continuous completion - the respondent does not complete the questionnaire all in one go. (You may have this as a condition either way.)
• Respondents not completing the questionnaire according to the instructions.
• Someone other than the respondent filling in the questionnaire.
• How many people's views are represented on the completed questionnaire. (The respondent might ask for other people's opinions before completing some questions.)

Ensuring that the questionnaire is filled in according to your requirements is practically impossible when it is done anywhere other than in your presence. Even getting respondents together in groups for this purpose is very costly in terms of time and money. One of the main reasons for choosing a questionnaire is its cost effectiveness, so you may be limited to a postal questionnaire or something similar. If this is the case, you can maximise the response rate by following these common-sense guidelines:

Note: Remember that everything about your questionnaire should be congruent with your research aims and method. So if you are asking someone to keep a diary, you may wish to steer clear of devices that make it seem too formal or official.

- How it looks.   Make it attractive.
  Make it easy to read.
  Provide good spaces for answers.
- How it arrives.   Send it to a named person, marked 'personal'.
  Send a stamped addressed envelope for return.
  Type addresses, etc. for 'official' look.
  Avoid franking and envelopes that look like adverts or 'junk' mail.
  Avoid holiday times, e.g. August and December.
  Are you sending it to a home or work address?
- Ensuring replies.   You could consider offering an incentive, e.g. a small 'gift' per completed questionnaire or the opportunity to win a prize in a draw.
  Details about incentives should go in the first mailing.
- If no reply.   Send a reminder.
  Say that you understand how busy your respondent is and that you appreciate and value their participation.
  Say that the research is important.
- If still no reply.   Don't give up, try another reminder.
  More than three reminders is a waste of time.

Developing a semi-structured questionnaire
Some researchers would not accept that there is any such thing as a semi-structured questionnaire. The point we are trying to make here, and indeed throughout this book, is don't be intimidated by the limited vision of others when it comes to qualitative methods. If you follow the planning and preparation process described in Chapter 2, you will develop a method with integrity.

There are few 'rules' governing the structure of questionnaires once you step outside the strict boundaries of quantitative, tightly structured questionnaires comprising weighted items that have been tested for reliability, validity, etc. Always remember that you are compromising between being able to manage the data flow in order to code and possibly even quantify your results, and collecting data that has the richness, spontaneity and natural quality you require. This is a difficult balance to strike.

When writing down questions and asking respondents to write their answers, you are limited to open and closed questions and the instructions which accompany them, see p.89. The following suggestions may be useful:

- The instructions are the key to a successful questionnaire. Plan carefully.
- Use simple straightforward language and a large, simple, easy-to-read typeface.
- Pilot the questions individually and the questionnaire as a whole.
- Use closed questions sparingly if you want to stick close to a qualitative style. All closed questions are 'forced choice' in that they give the respondent no flexible options. Here are some question types you might use:
  - A *Likert scale*: a numerical scale from 1 - 5 for example:
    How likely is it that you will change therapist in the next six months?

         1   2   3   4   5
    Highly improbable   Highly probable

  - A *semantic differential* scale: Asking respondents to decide between polar opposites in meaning:
    Put a cross on the scale to indicate what you think about your current therapist.

    Strong • • • • • • • • • Weak
    Kind   • • • • • • • • • Cruel
    Honest • • • • • • • • Dishonest
    Ethical • • • • • • • • Unethical

  - *Intensity measures*: How strongly do you feel about this? Followed by one of the above scales.

- *Don't know*: A mid point in a scale or a don't know option allows respondents to not answer with dignity. Quantitative methods try to prevent this from happening, but in a semi-structured questionnaire you may prefer to have this as an option in all cases.
- The received wisdom of questionnaire design instructs us to avoid open questions like the plague. In this case we do the opposite, throwing caution, and our need to tightly code the responses in numbers, to the wind.
- Consider giving respondents a fixed space to write their answers to open questions.

Diaries

You may ask your respondents to keep a diary focusing on a certain time period or sequence of events. You will need to take a careful approach to the planning of this method of collection. As with a questionnaire, the instructions are absolutely crucial and should be piloted before being used in the study proper.

- You might want to supply special forms on which the respondents are required to record the events and their thoughts and feelings. You will need to give as much attention to the layout and design of these forms as to any other type of semi-structured questionnaire.

- This method is particularly useful where people's experiences of intermittent periods of illness are sought, e.g. panic attacks. A log can be kept of when the attacks occur, an estimate of their duration and perceived severity. This basic information can then be supplemented by more detailed accounts of symptoms, thoughts and feelings accompanying the attacks.

- You could ask your respondents to keep a tape diary spoken into a small tape recorder which may even be used to record key events in the respondent's life. (Recent television shows have used narrative-style diary accounts of peoples' lives in programmes such as Video Diaries.)

Letters

Another even less structured data collection method is to write a letter to your selected respondents and ask them to write back detailing their experiences, opinions, thoughts and feelings. This is the least structured form of interrogation. You will nevertheless need to prepare for and plan the study, see pp.35-62 . A major set of decisions hinges upon how you choose the sample of people to whom you will write.

• Writing letters can be a more-or-less formal method, but if you wish to review your correspondence with other members of a political group from ten years ago, this falls into the category of a *trace method* (see p.108).

• A letter writing study is a 'live' study in the present time, e.g. you may start a letter-writing study today by writing to a sample of members of the British Association for Counselling about their experiences with clients' recovered memories.

• You could make first contact by placing an advert in a newspaper or specialist publication.

• Make sure that the people to whom you are writing (or have written) understand that they are taking part in a study. Get their permission before you use any of their material.

Interviews

At the risk of teaching our grandmothers to suck eggs, we'll see if counsellors have anything to learn about conducting interviews. It could be argued that counselling interviews have one function, that is roughly speaking to help the client in some way through an enabling process of self discovery. Interviews in qualitative research have a different prime function, that is to collect information in the form of opinions, feelings and attitudes (otherwise called *responses*) from the interviewee.

The differences between interviewing in qualitative research and quantitative research are that the qualitative interviewer:
• Recognises a wider range of responses as valid, e.g. free flowing speech, thoughts and feelings that appear to wander off the subject, anecdotes, etc.
• Understands the importance of relationship variables such as rapport between the researcher and the respondent.
• Sees the respondent as a whole person (hence recognising the validity of all of their responses - see above).
• May be only interviewing one person if the research is a single case study.
• May interview the respondent on more than one occasion, asking the same or different questions.
• May ask the respondent to collaborate more actively in the research by, for example, helping the researcher sort or categorise the responses.
• Will not be interested in counting or rating only a portion of responses as they are made, but will be more interested in taking a more complete record of all responses.
• May accept a wider range of possible interview techniques from asking pre-determined questions right through to unstructured exploration through helping the respondent reflect upon their experience (just as in counselling).

Planning an interview
As we explained above, interviews are not just a sequence of questions. Even interrogation of prisoners consists of a mixture of threats and promises in addition to questions! Counsellors will appreciate the importance of building a relationship with the person you are interviewing. Qualitative researchers call this *rapport* and also give the development of this quality a high priority. How do we combine the available interrogation and exploration skills into a sequence that builds rapport, and also make it a comfortable and

hopefully rewarding experience for the respondent which enables the researcher to collect the data they require?

Structure of an interview
The general structure of any interpersonal episode has a beginning, middle and end. Readers will be familiar with the structure of a typical counselling session and what the counsellor is trying to achieve as the session progresses. There are similarities between a counselling interview and a data collection interview. In a data collection interview these components have the following functions:

Beginning - introduce yourself to the respondent and build rapport (some people think of this as an opportunity to 'break the ice' or warm up). Set the boundaries appropriate to your interview, i.e. explain what the interview is about, how long it will take, whether you are offering confidentiality, how you will be recording the data (notes, audio, video).

Middle - this is the data collection and recording stage. Depending upon the type of interview, semi-structured or unstructured, this will follow a different pattern. You might consider starting with demographic information such as the name, age, etc. of the respondent, followed by some relatively less intrusive, superficial, or 'safe' questions, building to more intimate, deep, or 'risky' questions as the interview progresses. You may destroy the rapport you have established by clumsy, prematurely intimate or intrusive questioning early in the interview.

End - an abrupt end can be quite a shock after a searching interview. You will want to thank your respondent and reiterate any arrangements for subsequent interviews, ownership of the data, publication, confidentiality etc. This is both polite and gives you and your respondent the opportunity to 'wind down'. Counsellors are used to the 'door-knob' disclosures of clients where they get to the 'real' issues as they stand by the door on the way out. You may well find that your respondent does a similar thing whereby as you 'finish' the interview they start to tell you the most interesting and relevant material. Be prepared by having a strategy to capture this information - with the respondent's permission of course.

The setting of an interview

Readers will need only the briefest of reminders that interviews can take place in a variety of settings:
- In the respondent's home.
- As above at the respondent's place of work.
- A comfortable, private, quiet room, alone and face-to-face with the interviewer, at the interviewer's premises.
- As above but in a group.
- On the street - on the hoof, permission sought and granted on the spot.
- On the telephone - can be planned and arranged in advance or *ad hoc* with no appointment made. (Be ready for a refusal.)

Each setting will require different planning and preparation. Things to consider are:
- Distractions and interruptions.
- Confidentiality and privacy.
- The amount of time the interview will take (don't expect your respondents to stand in the street for half an hour).
- The type and quality of the data you wish to collect.
- How you are going to record the data.

Types of interview

Along with other data collection methods, interviews can also be placed on a dimension to describe their degree of structure. As with these other research methods, the more an interview has a pre-determined structure, the more researcher-centred it is. The less pre-determined the structure, the more respondent-centred it is. Qualitative researchers generally take a more respondent-centred approach to data collection. A qualitative research interview is more like a person-centred counselling interview, whereas a quantitative interview is more like a market research interview - rather like a questionnaire on legs.

Fully structured interview
These involve interrogation of the respondent's experience through pre-determined, researcher-determined, closed questions. Answers strictly coded for quantitative analysis of data. This quantitative approach is not covered by this book.

Semi-structured interview
The popular 'middle ground' in which interviewer has a clear agenda but uses 'softer' questions, more open questions, more conversational style, can move flexibly through the agenda by changing the order and emphasis of the questions depending upon the responses. This type of interview is favoured by those wishing to inject some qualitative more narrative material into an otherwise quantitative study. The style is a mixture of gentle interrogation and guided exploration.
Advantages - Bridges the 'gap' between qualitative and quantitative methods and can add support to the findings in either approach. Flexible yet allows the interviewer to control the flow of information.
Disadvantages - Moderately time consuming at data collection (because the interview has a semi-open ended quality and may be difficult to regulate the time) and data analysis (because the exploratory parts will generate lots of wordy unpredictable data).

How to conduct a semi-structured interview - the 'half-way-house' rather than a completely separate category of interview. The semi-structured interview represents a compromise which many researchers find comfortable. The skill of getting the researcher's agenda into the interview without applying a rigid schedule should be within the repertoire of most counsellors.

The first task is to plan an interview schedule which could start something like this:

1. Thank you for agreeing to take part in this survey. As I mentioned over the phone, I am conducting research into trainee counsellor's experiences in therapy. You also said that you would be happy to let me tape record the interview, does that still feel OK?
   If yes - Fine, in that case I'll set the recorder up and switch it on now. Continue at 2.
   If no - I appreciate you concerns. How do you feel about continuing with me taking notes?
      If yes - OK, are there any other questions you have before we start?
         If yes answer them and continue at 2.
         If no continue at 2.
      If no - I see. I realise that you have had more time to consider how you feel this interview since we spoke on the phone. Since I need to record the information in certain ways, it wouldn't be sensible for me to continue with the interview, so thanks for your time so far. Closing remarks.

2. The information you give is in the strictest confidence, you name will not be mentioned on the tape and you will get a chance to look at this work before it is submitted for publication if you wish. Any extracts from the tape will be worded so that you cannot be identified.

3. Firstly then, are you in therapy at the moment?

As can be seen in the example, the interview schedule is a mixture of aide-memoirs to help you if you dry up and instructions so that you know what to do next in order to get all the information you need. Use 'GOTO' instructions (sometimes called *skips*, i.e., 'if yes, skip to question 5') - 'If the answer to this question is yes, then GOTO question 5, if no, GOTO question 8.' And so on. Once the biographical and demographical information is collected at the beginning of the interview, you would proceed to collecting the main body of data:

7. *How did you choose your therapist when you started the course?*
Prompt *Was the choice made for you by the course tutors?*
Prompt *Was the therapist recommended to you?*
Prompt *Is their orientation the same as that of the course?*

8. *How far did you use the therapist to help deal with course issues?*
Prompt *Could you give me an example or two?*
If worried *Only go into as much detail as you feel comfortable with.*
Allow to develop and finish with *Is there any more you would like to tell me about that?*

The schedule allows you to stray from the path of the questions when you feel it is appropriate and yet it continues to remind you where you are up to, especially if each numbered item on it has a check-box next to it for you to tick when the question is asked. Because it encourages you to cover roughly the same ground with each respondent, this method holds the promise of a standardised procedure, without the straight-jacket feel of a completely structured interview. When the middle of the interview is complete, end the interview with some suitable closing remarks, including a sample of the wording in your schedule, see p.100.

Unstructured interview
In this type of interview the interviewer has no pre-determined agenda and no set questions to ask other than the research question or hypothesis they had to begin with. The interviewer style is exploratory and rather than ask closed questions they will guide and encourage the respondent with a few open questions and reflection. This type of interview may be called non-directive.

Advantages - Congruent with some therapeutic approaches. Respondents feel respected, listened to and involved. Very flexible indeed. Very rich source of information-packed data. *Disadvantages* - Very time consuming. Needs lots of good interview skills to be done well. Data analysis complex and again, very time consuming.

How to conduct an unstructured interview - now this really is trying to teach our grandmothers to suck eggs! An unstructured interview should be familiar territory for counsellors attempting person-centred, some psychodynamic, non-directive and various eclectic and integrative approaches. The one word of caution is to remember that you are a researcher and not a counsellor. Your objectives will be different and so the skills you employ will have to be appropriately different:
Your aim is to enable the respondent explore their experience and tell their story. You will need to focus their reflective process on the important elements in the story, the meaning of the elements for them, the feelings and thoughts that these elements evoke and any consequences or outcomes. You may want to attend carefully to any sequences of events etc, but if you are recording the interview on tape you will be freed from having to remember much of it apart from that which you need to facilitate further exploration.

Don't re-invent the wheel - there are several very good reasons for not developing your own interview schedule, not least the amount of work you save.
• It is always worth reviewing the literature to see if there is an interview with a question format that has been developed and successfully used by someone else. You will probably need their permission to use their material.
• In certain settings, it may be that the interviews have already been (or are already being) conducted wholly or in part. If your research involves a particular type of illness or set of predisposing factors you may find that you can use the clinical interviews of another practitioner. You may be able to use their records or tape-record the interviews as they continue

to see their clients routinely. Make sure that appropriate consent is sought and given.
• The Repertory Grid approach (see p.111) has generated distinct methods of developing interview schedules. There are several good accounts of the basic principles, e.g. Fransella and Bannister (1977).
• Q-methodology (see p.115) developed by Stephenson (1953) suggests certain conventions for question asking which might be appropriate for your study. For a good account see Butler and Haigh (1954).
• Interpersonal Process Recall or IPR (see p.113) is a personal awareness raising and relationship development method originated by Norman Kagan in the late 1960s (e.g. Kagan and Krathwohl 1967 and more recently Kagan 1984). It involves the protagonists in an interpersonal interaction (group, dyad, formal or informal) reviewing a record of the interaction (video or audiotape) in a loosely structured yet quite particular way with the help of a specially trained interviewer or *inquirer*. IPR has been used as a research tool to evaluate experiences in a number of ways, a straightforward account is given by Marsh (1983).

Compare and Contrast # 5
(Structure and Control)

Readers may have noticed that along with the dimension of structure, comes the dimension of control. We believe that control is exerted through structure, although some books refer to interviews, for example, in terms of who is in control, the interviewer or the interviewee.

This returns to one of the fundamental differences between quantitative and qualitative philosophies, namely the problem of data management. Human data is chaotic and unruly. We can take one of two opposing views about this: That these qualities are either difficult (quantitative) or exciting (qualitative). The view that we take then affects how we deal with this chaos: we either try to manage, tame, regulate and otherwise control our data (quantitative), or facilitate, develop, nurture, and otherwise elaborate our data.

The qualitative way is clear - enhancement and facilitation of data flow, not control. This position has a fundamental affect on the organisation of qualitative work and the collection of qualitative data.

III Looking at what's left behind

Wherever human beings have been, we find evidence of their lives in a number of forms. We leave our mark by either adding to the environment or removing something from it. We leave behind us a trail, elements of which endure to different degrees. This trail can be followed, to determine the effect that humans have had on history, the world and each other. A familiar example of this trail-following research is archaeology but although social science researchers might go 'digging' around in archives and litter-bins, there are few similarities save painstakingly methodical procedures.

Looking at what's left behind in the wake of human living can provide data that supports other findings for the purposes of triangulation, or can offer a parallel narrative strand to illuminate other work, or occasionally can be a valid research method in its own right. The use of documents and quotations is well known in the social sciences, less so is the use of physical 'remainders'. Some recent social science research has made creative use of the various debris of human life, but any use of physical traces in counselling research would need to be even more creative. However the material is used, it does not offer an easy route to cast-iron answers. The collection and collation methods involve painstaking and diligent searching, rigorous scrutiny and disciplined analysis. Do not underestimate the time and effort involved.

The human trail is divided into two broad categories - that which we have left in terms of additions to the world - products and the like, and the marks of destruction and removal of material from the world. These are called *accretion measures* and *erosion measures* respectively.

Documents and records
By these, we mean official documents and records in both the public and private or personal domains. Official records, e.g. Hansard, minutes of public meetings, company memos, letters, etc. These may be of limited interest to counsellors. We can, however imagine the history of the struggles to establish and keep a counselling service in a college being understood through content analysis of academic board papers. Local government provision for people with mental health problems could be elucidated by looking at council minutes.

Published media
Documents such as books, newspapers, magazines, advertisements etc. The history of therapy and counselling in the published media has been the subject of at least idle interest. Content analysis (see p.130) of journal articles could be used to understand gender bias, white anglo-centricitry and other issues. For a good account of action research in the published media see Miller (1993).

Broadcast media
Television, radio, film, video, recorded speech and music etc. We might be interested in looking at the representation of counselling in the media; views of counselling in the popular press, how often the word 'counselling' is said on *News at Ten* and in what context, or images of counsellors in film. For a good account of action research in the broadcast media see Miller (1993).

Physical traces
Any physical addition to, or erosion of, the environment, including the infrastructure of human society as it impacts upon the natural world. This may seem of little relevance or use as far as counselling is concerned, but at a stretch we could imagine being interested in the contents of the litter-bins in counsellors' offices or the patterns of carpet wear in and out of the various sections of a student services suite in an further education college.

Sampling the data

As with all methods, we have to decide which parts of the data (in these methods it's more like 'evidence') we are going to use. In other words how we are going to sample the data. Although each type of data suggests some sampling techniques and strategies that are more sensible than others, there are no rules to help you decide how to sample the data. You may, however, want to consider the following commonsense guidelines:

- Does your data suggest that you sample by time, event, person, or place?
- Is there anything that might bias your sampling, e.g. availability of material, your own preferences, etc? If so be sure to declare any biases.
- Sample only as much data as you can handle.
- Remember that if you don't get it right first time, most of this data is durable and will be still waiting for you at a later date.

IV Other Methods

Repertory Grid techniques

Repertory Grid techniques have grown out of the personality theory proposed by George Kelly (1955) called *personal construct theory*. Kelly thought that the key to understanding what lay behind people's actions was to look at how they constructed and interpreted their personal worlds. He proposed that people continually develop theories about the world and interpret their experiences in the light of these theories. This was not a new idea, even in 1955, but what was new was that Kelly applied the notion to the *social* and *personal* worlds of people. (Previously it has been suggested that people might form and test hypotheses about how we saw the world of objects, but not how we understand the world of feelings and interactions with others.)

It was Kelly's view that the theories which people form are a set of bipolar ideas or *constructs* such as cruel - kind, aggressive - gentle. Kelly's most important point was that everyone has their own set of unique personal constructs. We make up our own. This all makes personal construct theory an attempt to model and explain the phenomenological basis of individual personality. The method that Kelly developed for getting at, or eliciting, these personal constructs from people, and showing how we use them to interpret our experience, is called *Repertory Grid technique*.

The basic repertory grid technique itself consists of the following stages:
   1. Identifying the group of participants in the study, e.g. *counsellors* or *clients*, possibly belonging to a particular agency.

2. Repertory grid is a technique that is formulated for each participant individually, so for each participant:
    i. Naming a set of 'elements' which depend upon the focus of the particular study in question, e.g. if the research topic was *counselling,* or *interpersonal relationships* then the elements would be people who are significant in the life of the person being studied, maybe counsellors, friends and relatives.
    ii. Taking these elements in groups of three, the person is asked to say in what way any two is different from the third. E.g. my counsellor is different from my brother and mother because she is a more challenging person.
    iii. These are arranged in grid form to explore the emerging personal constructs.

An excellent practical guide to repertory grid work is given by Fransella and Bannister (1977). A computer will make analysis of the grids much easier if you are dealing with more than a couple of participants. In a large group, with many constructs a computer is practically essential if you are to extract the underlying constructs. The field of personal construct psychology and repertory grid techniques is filled with lively debate over such issues as whether it is best to stay with the idiosyncratic constructs generated by each individual, or whether to use ready-made constructs provided by the researcher. (You can, after all, only get out what you put in.)

There are many examples of repertory grid techniques in the research literature, e.g. Winter (1967) who looked at the effects of social skills training. When the personal constructs of the participants in a social skills training programme emerged, it turned out that those who failed to benefit from the programme did not learn social skills because they did not want to, rather than because they were not able to. Analysis of their personal constructs revealed that they associated social skills with negative attributes such as dishonesty and selfishness, and so they resisted the training.

Interpersonal Process Recall

Developed by Norman Kagan in the 1960s, Interpersonal Process Recall (IPR) is a semi-structured method of eliciting story-telling from the actors in a dyad or group. It has the potential of revealing deep feelings and so does require careful consideration before being used. It also requires that the action in question has been recorded either on video or audio tape. The story-telling or *recall* is facilitated by a trained interviewer called an *inquirer*. The data elicited by the inquirer can itself be recorded on audio or video for subsequent analysis.

The technique, outlined by Kagan in several publications, e.g. Kagan (1984) involves the participants watching on video, or listening to on audiotape, the action in question. They are asked to stop the tape whenever they remember anything about what was going on at the time. The inquirer helps them 'tell their story' by asking a series of semi-structured open questions and prompts such as:

'Were there any feelings associated with what you said? What were the feelings?'
'Was this a familiar sensation? When has it happened before?'
'What did you think the others were thinking at that moment?'
'Describe any images that flashed in front of your eyes when you did that'

The 'rules' are simple -
- Stay in the *there and then*.
- Stick to recalling your own (i.e. the 'recaller's' own) stuff.
- The 'recaller' has control over the process and can decline to answer.
- The 'recaller' can start and stop the tape wherever they choose.

The recall can be done individually or in pairs or groups (there are benefits to doing both group and individual recall). If recall is done in groups, interactions during the recall sessions, whilst very profitable in terms of yielding good data, must be managed carefully or the process from the *there and then* will start up again in the *here and now*.

IPR has been used to a limited extent as a research tool, e.g. Marsh (1983) who used it to look at the meaning of 'boredom' on a training course. IPR helped elaborate the simple idea that boredom is a automatically a bad thing, to a series of issues for the trainer to address. It is our view that IPR is under-used as a research tool in qualitative studies. It seems admirably suited to creative development as a method of reflection and learning.

Meta Analysis

Whenever there is a large number of studies on a particular topic, it makes sense to attempt to reach some overall conclusions based on this body of work. There are perhaps three ways we might use the efforts of other researchers. We could review the literature, and indeed we would do this by way of introducing any study, qualitative or quantitative. We could use the data from some or all of the work to carry out further or secondary analysis to reach further or secondary conclusions. Our third option is meta analysis.

Meta analysis is an analysis of a series of results whereby trends, regularities and patterns are sought. It is a method used more frequently in quantitative study, but there in no reason why the principle cannot be adapted to qualitative work. Meta analysis is not simply a literature review, it seeks to go further in the sense that it tries to identify fundamental strands or factors, and hence an overall conclusion. It might, for example, be useful to apply meta analysis to the research on the effects of counselling. Such an analysis would be quantitative if the original data is quantitative. Advanced statistical methods used with the help of microcomputers are almost essential for quantitative meta analysis.

Recent attempts to develop qualitative meta analysis include Noblitt and Hare (1988).

Q-Methodology
Developed by Stephenson (1953), Q-Methodology is a technique in which the respondent is asked to sort through cards containing self-referent statements. The sort is repeated and progressive and the respondent sorts successively using different criteria. From the final positions of the cards in the sort it is possible to measure how an individual perceives or rates their self-concept.

The technique is used most frequently with individuals to get some idea of changes in self-perception. This is just as well since the analysis becomes very complex with large numbers. Stephenson (1980) describes using Q-sorting with a four year old girl who was asked to sort cards in terms of dimensions such as 'most like me', 'most like me according to my mother,' etc. The technique has certain resonances with repertory grid technique, described earlier.

Counsellors may have come across Q-methodology as described by Carl Rogers. He gives a number of accounts in different places, most accessibly in *On Becoming A Person* (1961) in which describes his application of the method to measure change in a client in some detail, see Rogers (1961) pages 232-241. The treatment of Q-sort data can be quantitative or qualitative, as described by Rogers. Q-methodology is another under-utilised approach to research which is sufficiently adaptable to be used in qualitative research in the area of counselling and therapy.

Action Research
Combining the 'action' and 'participation' and 'collaboration' themes of qualitative study, action research is research rooted in everyday life. Proposed by Kurt Lewin in the 1940s and described later (Lewin 1951) it found favour amongst sociologists and social scientists looking at interpersonal and group behaviour. Not simply doing research *about* everyday issues, the action researcher *actively intervenes* in live social situations to see what will happen. Such interventions can be planned and pre-determined or spontaneous, although most that get published tend to be thought through to a greater extent.

Action research can be large-scale (government or pressure group sponsored media campaigns to combat AIDS or stop smoking), or small scale (small group interventions). The common feature in all action research is that the protagonists do not know what the outcome of the intervention will be (the 'action' component). The effects are measured in some way - that is the 'research' component.

Some action researchers see themselves in a romantic light as mavericks, adopting a 'guerilla-research' approach employing surprise tactics and sailing close to the edge in terms of ethics. Some research ethical issues by deliberately crossing ethical boundaries. A good account of action research is given by Miller (1993) who documents many interventions, presenting some as escapades or 'scams', notably her production of street-press newspapers at media and group-relations conferences.

5 Treating Qualitative Data

Some people find it difficult to imagine how to analyse data without quantifying it in some way. In fact the very word *data* brings numbers to mind. There is a further problem which we have tried to address in the chapter heading. We have challenged the assumption that the only thing that can be done with data (or the only thing that researchers will be interested in) is to *analyse* it. This notion will confuse another group of readers. What else can you do with data other than analyse it?

Some useful questions.
What is data?
This is not the first time we have asked this question, and tried to answer it in this book. On page 64 in Chapter 4 we tackled this issue in order to help us identify the sort of information we might be collecting in a qualitative study. The answer now is much the same as it was then - qualitative data is just about anything you can think of that lies within the realm of human experience, whether or not (with some emphasis on the 'or not') it can be put into numbers. Data is what you have collected.

What is our data?
Now this question is looking at what we have actually ended up with. It is important to consider this for a moment so that we can move towards deciding upon what method of treatment might be most appropriate. The answer to the question partly depends upon how it has been collected and recorded.

What can be done with data?
In Chapter 1 we described how qualitative researchers view the issues of data and data treatment. A summary of the points we made then could be used as a set of principles of qualitative data treatment as follows:

The principles of qualitative data treatment.
• We are interested in the natural patterns in data and consider these to be of more intrinsic value than any artificial enhancement or amplification.
• We prefer to use treatments which involve humans as the instruments of treatment rather than mechanistic tests or numerical models. We seek to preserve the human quality in the data treatment by using treatments that are congruent and in harmony with both the data itself and ourselves as human instruments.
• We understand that process and outcome are the same in qualitative data treatment. *The process of qualitative data treatment is the outcome.*
• In our search for patterns and qualities in our data rather than numbers and quantities, we will seek and develop novel and innovative treatment methods based on subjective and intuitive processes of synthesis in addition to more traditional processes of analysis.

If these are the principles, then next we will turn to the themes of qualitative data treatment. These themes emerge in different individual techniques and methods of treatment. Some methods are simple expressions of one theme, whilst other methods are a combination of themes.

Synthesis: This is the putting together of information to arrive at new understanding. By adding information, or recombining it in novel ways, we synthesise some new patterns and meanings. This process is particularly good for understanding interactions between things. The study of human beings is more often than not the study of interactions, so some believe that synthesis, or making combinations and associations between information, is particularly useful in the study of human action.

Analysis: More familiar to most of us is the process of taking something apart to understand it better or find meaning in it. This method is familiar to us when trying to diagnose why something mechanical or electrical isn't working, e.g. a washing machine or car.

Elaboration: This is the technique of extending, continuing, developing, embellishing or enhancing something until we find meaning in it. This is a little like completing a dot-to-dot picture or doing some painting by numbers. The basic pattern is there but we can only really make sense of it by further embellishment or elaboration. We may do this by adding extra material, possibly of our own.

Description: Often seen as a first stage of data treatment in quantitative studies, but can be the whole of data treatment in a number of circumstances. In qualitative research, describing data is seen as a highly skilled, illuminating and valid method of data treatment. Description is not simply writing about what has happened. There are many creative forms of description, many requiring careful preparation and discipline.

Reflection: At the unstructured end of data treatment is a reflective process where the researcher, though a 'tuned instrument', eschews any structured approach to data treatment. They still seek the same features in the data such as patterns, regularities and so forth, but do so through a process of deliberation and meditation that is at best semi-systematic.

Repetition: I can remember being told at school that I would do a particular piece of maths work over and over again until I got it right. Not quite in the same spirit, we may choose to repeat a type of data treatment to see what happens. Let's say we chose to categorise our data in a certain way at the beginning of our data treatment. Then, one month later we decide to do it all over again. We may find that the results of the second categorisation are the same as the first or different. Either way, we have learned something.

Time and timing
The idea of repeating the same data treatment technique over and over serves to remind us of one very important fact in qualitative research: *Data treatment takes time.* More than this, it needs to take time in the same sense that a good wine needs time to mature, we might even see laying our data aside for a while (to let it 'mature') as another valid treatment method.

Then there is the further issue of when the treatment of the data takes place. There is general agreement that data treatment can take place before, during and after collection. The timing of data treatment has a strong effect on the overall flavour of the research. The more pre-determined the data treatment method is, the more quantitative in style the study becomes.

• Pre-determined data treatment - this is the hallmark of structured, quantitative research. The data treatment is fixed before collection and therefore relatively inflexible. It is often fixed with a theory in mind or a hypothesis springing from a theory. Either way the effort is directed towards collecting evidence for a pre-determined purpose, usually to support or refute an idea.
• Data treatment during collection - this can be researcher-directed or collaborative. It requires a more flexible schedule and almost inevitably leads to modified aims or avenues of exploration and inquiry from those originally planned.
• Data Treatment after collection - can be determined by an original pre-determined plan, collaboration with participants at the end of the data collection period, or the result of data treatment during the study.

The last two data treatment occasions are more frequently (if not exclusively) associated with qualitative research and as such may be of more interest to readers. However, just because pre-determined data treatment is presented here as a sign of quantitative methods, firstly it doesn't have to be on every occasion and secondly that does not mean that qualitative researchers shouldn't *plan* their data treatment as much as possible before doing it (usually this means before the collection stage). This plan will, of course be flexible and open to modification as a result of data collection and treatment as the study progresses.

Compare and Contrast # 6
(Theory and where it comes from)

It is obvious that theories do not emerge out of thin air. Even on those rare occasions when a person has a 'flash of inspiration' there is usually a helpful context which goes some way to explaining the origin of the idea, (like an apple falling on someone's head, or water overflowing from a bath). It is the unique blend of context and person that generates the hypothesis that leads to the theory.

In quantitative work, theory can be generated in a number of ways, a feature which can be that theory is imported from outside of the situation to which it is being applied. In other words it is taken out of context. This is particularly true when ideas are generalised from one small situation to human situations as a whole. It is a feature of qualitative work that experience be contextualised, so it follows that theory should be too.

Glaser and Strauss (1967) advocated an unstructured approach to observations of human action, and went further to outline how theory might emerge from and be grounded in the phenomena studied. They called this *Grounded Theory*, and their recipe for this emergent theory is firstly that observers should enter a research situation with no prior theoretical preconceptions, and secondly they should create, refine and revise theory in the light of data collected.

Grounded hypotheses, generated in this way should be more 'true to life' than those generated out of a decontextualised commitment to a theory such as Personal Construct Theory, Behaviourism or Psychoanalytic Theory. Development of grounded theory depends upon an unstructured, flexible, participative and collaborative style.

Methods of data treatment

Signs of successful, sound data treatment are, firstly that it is planned, secondly that it is congruent and in harmony with the aims of the research, the collection methods, and the data itself, and thirdly that it combines more than one theme. So the data will be *described* and *elaborated,* or perhaps *reflected upon* before being *analysed.*

We will now list and explain a range of data treatment methods and techniques. The list is as full as we could make it without needlessly splitting hairs. Although it's our best effort it is bound to be incomplete. There will be, no doubt, some method lurking in the literature that will become the next 'big thing'. This is the exciting thing about qualitative methods - new approaches, new ways and new techniques are developing all the time. This should be encouraging to beginning researchers, since in essence there is no reason why you should develop a novel method that suits *your* data.

The list is an attempt to give you some reference points and starting points. Do bear in mind however, that qualitative research has a strong collaborative theme. By this we mean not only collaborating with your participants, but also with fellow researchers and supervisors. Seek out someone experienced to help with your data treatment. Preferably someone who knows a little about the area on which your project focuses. We have already strongly suggested that you find a supervisor for your research. Now it is essential.

Coding

Codes are any device used to attach values to events in research. This usually means using numbers in some way or other, but in qualitative research we should not think of numbers as the first or only coding possibility. So what else can we use as codes and how do we go about the task of coding our data?

Note: In fact the whole of this chapter is about coding, different methods of coding for different circumstances, some very general, some highly stylised. The purpose of this section is twofold, firstly to give some idea of the types of activity that are traditionally used as coding practices, and secondly to give ourselves permission to do whatever is appropriate and works for us regardless of what others have done in the past. Like all other areas of qualitative endeavour, there are no 'rules', save commitment to quality through a thoughtful, patient and rigorous application of commonsense, plus our best attempt to preserve the humanness in our studies through practice that is congruent with our nature.

Coding is done to reduce data to manageable proportions. It is a way of allocating values via some sort of abbreviation or symbol, e.g. single words (as in typologies), letters of the alphabet (as in categories), or numbers (at this point the analysis becomes quantitative). We have already mentioned coding in the context of questionnaires and interviews. In that case, the codes allocated to responses were pre-determined and therefore part of the data collection method rather than a data treatment method. Pre-determined coding also has the effect of imposing considerable structure on your data collection, so we considered it to be leaning quite strongly towards a model mixed with quantitative methods. Coding doesn't have to be pre-determined though - it can also be responsive or even collaborative.

Coding done after all the data has been collected is more flexible and can be developed in response to the changing requirements of the study as the data is collected, or in response to collaboration between the researcher and participants. Collaboration is particularly valuable if *indigenous categories* are being used (see below p.125) since only the participants can usefully attach values to them in any coding scheme. Existing coding schemes (devised by others) can be used alongside coding schemes developed specially for the study in hand.

Since the purpose of coding is to *manage* data, the act of applying a code to data always reduces its complexity or changes it in some way. This is one of the basic arguments against quantitative methods, namely that applying numbers to human data is too restrictive, changes the nature of the data, is incongruent with 'human' data and oversimplifies complex processes. The trouble is, we find exactly the same problem in qualitative coding. All coding or data treatment methods become a trade off between presenting very complex human data in an easily assimilated form, and the unacceptable limitations, oversimplifications and distortions that are necessary to achieve this. Each coding or data treatment method will be assessed (where appropriate) for its degree of distortion/oversimplification as it is presented.

The degree of elaboration in coding depends upon the data collection method. In its simplest form coding is the description of events in words or prose, next comes the naming of categories and so on. At the other extreme it consists of developing elaborate schemes for allocating numbers to responses to questionnaire items or interview questions. There is no set method or procedure, successful coding is the product of commonsense, thoughtful planning and where possible, collaboration and careful piloting of the scheme.

Describing
Along with categorisation, description is probably the most frequently used data treatment method. Readers may be wondering how *simply* describing something could be called data *treatment* when it doesn't appear to actually *treat* the data in any way. As we have outlined above, description *is* a coding method since the action (behaviour, thoughts or feelings) have to be translated into words. This is coding of a sort, and most often the action is described by a third party (the researcher) who is not an actor. So, we have included description as a method of data treatment for the above and following reasons:
- Firstly description isn't simple. There are different styles which can be adopted, some dependent upon the position of the researcher in relation to the action, e.g:
    - narrative accounts - telling the story based on a sequence of events, either as a participant oneself or from the viewpoint of other participants.

- journalistic accounts - more external to the action, possibly as a non, or less participant, observer.
- Secondly description isn't transparent or neutral. It does interfere with, change or *treat* the data in some way. A descriptive account is filtered through the person doing the describing, so in that important sense there is a strong element of self-conscious data treatment.

Description is usually used alongside other forms of data treatment. It is, however a mistake to see it simply as a method of data presentation. In order to describe something we have to adopt a viewpoint from which to describe. This immediately changes or contextualises the description and should be recognised as a data treatment agent.

Advantages: The most flexible, least obtrusive data treatment method, offering the fewest opportunities for distortion or limitation of data. It is capable of acknowledging the full complexity of the data.

Disadvantages: May not limit the data enough for some purposes - is longwinded and doesn't 'manage' the data very well for simple presentation.

Categorising

Categorising things is at the heart of qualitative methodology, so it would be surprising if it were not represented as a data treatment method. There is no magic in categorisation, simply the application of common sense and a systematic, well prepared procedure. Two broad types of category emerge:

- Indigenous categories - those 'naturally occurring' categories used by the participants themselves in the situation under study. It is essential to the sensitive understanding of the action for the researcher to elicit these categories at some point during the research. Indigenous categories shape and determine the action and the participants' meanings in a number of ways. E.g. a year group of college students may categorise themselves as 'crusties', 'hippies', 'townies', 'techno-freaks' or whatever.

- Researcher categories - those categories imposed on the action or data by the researcher according to some principle determined before, during or after the collection of the data. Such researcher categories may be determined by:
  - a theoretical perspective,
  - the action or data as it comes in to influence the researcher,
  - a reflective process within the researcher,
  - a collaborative process involving the participants, but where the categories are still largely imported from a frame of reference external to the action.

So, the same college year group might be divided by the researcher into, for example:
- demographic categories such as age, gender, ethnic origin, socio-economic grouping etc,
- friendship categories as a result of a sociographic analysis of their relationships,
- categories based on experiences such as those who attend counselling sessions and those who do not.

The type of categories used in any study will depend upon the particular data treatment method chosen. Categorisation as a basic technique is pandemic in qualitative research. It's usually just a question of *how* you're going to do it, not *whether* you're going to do it. In each of the methods below there is an expression of categorisation, often stylised to meet the needs of the data or theoretical perspective of the research.

Useful categories are ones that make life easy for the researcher. To some extent this should be under our control in the case of researcher categories. If we want to make things easy for ourselves we should aim for categories that are mutually *exclusive* and *exhaustive*, i.e. ensuring that there is no overlap between categories, or that one piece of data cannot fall in two categories and that no data is left uncategorised at the end. These features are impossible to guarantee in indigenous categories. In fact it may be an essential feature of an indigenous category system that is permits flexibility, overlapping and movement between categories.

Exclusivity and exhaustiveness are always to be aimed for when planning the category and coding system, and should be checked out for 'water tightness' during piloting of the category system.

Advantages: Indigenous categories offer the least interference, distortion and limitation of the data in a category system. They honour the participants' meanings in their experience. Aids simple presentation and helps understanding through sensitive simplification.
Disadvantages: Can get too complex. If researcher's categories are used they can get 'out of sync' with the participants' experience. Begins to simplify the experience of others to a point which easily becomes inaccurate or offensive.

Sorting
Sorting is what you do to your data when you've got your categories worked out. Like sorting cards into suits, data is sorted into categories. In fact the process can be identical if, as was popular before the advent of computers (see Compare and Contrast# 7 on p.134), the researcher writes units of data on cards and sorts them into piles.

We have seen above how the categories into which the data is sorted are devised. The sorting process itself can be done according to sets of 'rules' determined by a number of factors, ranging from those determined by theory to those determined by the intuition of the researcher. The only requirement is that the method be identified, acknowledged and documented.

Typologies
Some researcher-generated systems of categorisation are more 'sophisticated' than others. When a multi-dimensional or matrix-style category system is developed, it is sometimes called a typology. Although the names given to the 'types' within a typology are entirely arbitrary, the nodes on the matrix, or multiple categories are

presented in such a way as to imply that they are *naturally occurring* features of the data that emerge after an initial sorting. We believe that such an implication is very misleading, since no types are 'naturally occurring' at all, they are artefacts produced by the researchers manipulation of the data and the names given to the types are metaphors or analogues, often with a mythological or populist double-entendre. More complex typologies create a matrix of types by having categories which overlay each other.

An example of a typology which embodies the points above is described by Maccoby (1979), reported in many publications such as Handy (1985) and concerns so-called 'corporate types'. These types were 'identified' by Maccoby after studying 250 managers in American organisations. They are:

> The Jungle Fighter   The Company Man
> The Gamesman   The Craftsman

We will leave readers to use their imagination to apply descriptions to each type, since in our view they will be as valid as anything Maccoby has been able to come up with. The same criticisms can, in our view, be levelled at other 'famous' typologies, including those favoured by counsellors and therapists, e.g. Jung's archetypes or Berne's typology of interactions (games) etc.

Advantages: Help illuminate data. Are simple to use.
Disadvantages: Reduce the complexity of humanity to discrete
>   units by using plausible metaphors. Prone to offensive oversimplification of experience. The plausibility is more a comment on our need to categorise things to make them easy to understand rather than actual features of the data. We tend to easily 'force' behaviour into a type, once we know what the type is.

Using time: chronologies
Chronological analysis is, as the name suggests, a time-dependent way of organising or categorising the data. There are two basic

ways of using time in a research project, either longitudinal or cross-sectional.
- Longitudinal - where data is collected from a single source over time, e.g. following a single person or group through a period of time (weeks, months, years), or a single record such as the minutes of a planning group for weeks, months, years. A particular form of longitudinal study used in qualitative work is a life history approach. These are auto biographical accounts of the whole of a person's life (rather than 'key moments' or 'turning points') in narrative form.
- Cross sectional - where data is collected from many different cohorts (to represent different ages in a process) at a single moment in time, e.g. looking at 5, 7 and 9 year olds at a particular school one September or taking the minutes from several planning groups that are currently at different stages in their life-cycle.

Arranging events in order of time also helps draw out some features in the data which might otherwise have been missed. There are some time-related data features which can be better demonstrated in a chronological sequence:
- Historical legacy - where the weight of past events shapes present expectations.
- Developmental effects - changes over time.
- Temporal association - where two events happen so closely together that we can make a reasonable assumption that they may be causally related, e.g. although I've never seen the electricity in a wire, I assume that the flicking of the switch caused the light bulb to illuminate because they happen so closely together in time.
- Temporal projection - predicting future events by projecting current sequences of events into the future.

When researchers, quantitative or qualitative are dealing with time, they are often looking for some kind of pattern to emerge over time. If it is possible to arrange data in a time sequence or series, these patterns sometimes emerge. If this approach is scaled up to use multiple data collections any patterns in the data stand a greater chance of revealing themselves. It is always worth using as much data as possible when looking for possible patterns over time, since the cumulative effect of the layers of data is what reveals the patterns.

Advantages: Time is a natural feature, so arranging things in order of time will not distort events or oversimplify them to a great degree. Helps structure events in an understandable way.
Disadvantages: Can lead to spurious links, e.g. temporal associations might lead us to make causal links where there are none, i.e. build an idea on coincidences.

Content analysis
All kinds of media data, from documents to video, can be subjected to content analysis. The main areas of interest in the social sciences concern mass media, i.e. newspapers, magazines, advertisements, photographs, television, radio, and films. However, the use of content analysis does not have to be limited to these 'mainstream' media. Minutes of meetings, letters, and speeches all have been subjected to content analysis to some limited degree. The approach has also been used on questionnaire and interview items, and response content.

Content analysis itself is the systematic analysis of the content of the media document in question. Various 'specialist' versions of content analysis have been adapted and developed for use in different situations with different media documents. We will consider one such specialist application in detail; discourse analysis, see p.136.

Carrying out a content analysis is a straightforward procedure requiring time, patience and an orderly approach to categorisation. Assuming you have:
- developed your research question,
- decided on your method and
- found and assembled the media you want to study,

we suggest the following simple guidelines:

Sampling: As with almost every other method, one of the first tasks is to have a sampling strategy. In the case of content analysis, the purpose is to limit the flow of data to manageable proportions. For detail on sampling see Sanders and Liptrot 1993, pp.70-76.

Typically, the useful questions involve firstly which factor will determine the sampling, e.g. time/date, person, event or place, and secondly what type of sampling method will be used, e.g. random, stratified, opportunity, etc. Each type of media will suggest appropriate sampling strategies, e.g. television programmes may be best sampled randomly over time - a random sample of ten *Newsnight* programmes over a six month period.

It may be necessary to have second or third stages in a sampling strategy, to continue with our example; we may then stratify the sample of *Newsnight* programmes so that all items are proportionally represented in our sample. Our final sampling stage will be to take segments of text from the programme (including or excluding visuals?) e.g. a two minute segment, one minute into each item and every two minutes thereafter according to the length of the item.

Units of record: Now we have to decide what it is we are looking for and recording. Again, each type of media will suggest certain units of record. In a television programme we can choose from sentences, phrases and words spoken to camera, words in voice-over, moving images - live action, video footage, archive footage, still images, background music, all of this can be in the programme proper or the title sequence. We could record the number or type of whole items, programme segments, length of time spent on each item and so on. There are many variations and decisions are likely to be far from simple since each one will affect the nature of the material collected.

If we were looking at newspapers we might use as our unit of record the number of times the word 'counselling' appeared, the size of the headline when counselling is the topic, the number of words in the article or whatever.

Context issues: Although content analysis is, fairly obviously concerned with content, there is more than passing acknowledgement of the context in which the unit of record occurs. If we have chosen individual words as the unit of record, we know that the meaning of a word is entirely dependent upon the rest of the sentence, paragraph, page, article, book etc. We would not draw the same conclusions from seeing the word 'counsellor' 20 times in a tabloid newspaper under different headlines:
> *Counsellors sold drugs to school children.*
> *Counsellor saved my dog from drowning.*
> *Counsellor awarded MBE for famine relief charity work.*
> *Counsellors to help hostages recover from trauma.*

Only one of these headlines has something to do with counsell*ing*. We would be further interested in whether the context had a positive, favourable or negative, unfavourable effect on the meaning of the word.

There are other contextual factors which must be taken into consideration such as:
- What authority does the recorded material have (who said or wrote or sponsored it?).
- Where is it published, broadcast, etc?

Determine the categories: The task of constructing categories has been covered on p.126, where the general principles have been outlined. The trouble with categorisation is that it is almost entirely situation and research-question specific. There is a huge range of possible categories that can be used in content analysis. Following on from the section on context, when constructing categories we must remember to consider not only the content but also:
- Whether the meaning is favourable or unfavourable, positive or negative.
- What overall goals the media might espouse.
- What values are ascribed to or revealed by the media, its methods or the item(s) under study.

As mentioned on p.127, categories in research, both qualitative and quantitative, should really be exclusive and exhaustive. Although these features are something to aim for in general, they can only really be checked out in practice by piloting the category system, see below.

Pilot the categories: Again, the purpose and strategy of piloting has been covered earlier on p.48. In content analysis along with other methods in qualitative work, we would test the appropriateness, accuracy and trustworthiness of our data treatment method by collaborating with others.

Do the analysis proper: this means do whatever systematic acts of categorisation you have planned as part of your content analysis. There are devices which can be used as aids to the content analysis categorisation process. These can be either manual or computerised:
- Frequency counts - counting the number of times a word or phrase, (or even a category) for example, occurs in a given text. These can be expressed in two basic ways:
  - *key word counts* - the frequencies of key or target words,

    e.g. | Counsellor | 36 |
    |---|---|
    | Counselling | 76 |
    | Psychotherapist | 12 |
    | Psychotherapy | 16 |
    | Alcoholism | 32 |
    | Drug abuse | 53 |
    | Tranquillizer dependency | 17 |

  - *ranked frequencies of occurrence* - in order of most frequent to least frequent, regardless of relevance to the study in hand, e.g.

Case	79
Debt	79
College	78
Counselling	76
Science	75

Such lists can be compared between documents or media or to 'absolute measures' such as official word counts which give the naturally-occurring frequencies of words in various media. If category counts are being used, these will automatically be 'key categories' since it would be foolish to develop and include categories which have no meaning for your study!

• Context lists - Key word in context (KWIC) lists give the list of contexts in which the key or target words occur, e.g. the five words preceding and five words following the key word. These can be expressed as frequency counts as above, and the researcher chooses the extent of the context and any omissions. These will alert the researcher to any phrases which, once identified, can lead to further analysis.

• Multiple criteria lists - listing those instances when a case (word, phrase or category event) meets more than one criterion at the same time. This can become complicated and time consuming and such multiple and combined category analyses are fast becoming the sole domain of computers.

Advantages: Has a 'natural' appeal in that it seems a commonsense form of analysis to most people. Is a flexible form of data treatment since the coding element can be made more or less structured and complex. Same other advantages as categorisation.
Disadvantages: Is an involved, disciplined procedure. Time and other resource consuming. Same other disadvantages as categorisation.

Compare and Contrast # 7
(Computers and automation)

For many years, computers were exclusively associated with mathematical and statistical calculations or 'number-crunching' applications. This meant that the application of automation and computers in social science research was limited to quantitative methods. Whilst it is still the case that quantitative study, particularly the statistical treatment of data, is considerably helped - and in some cases only made possible - by the use of computers, qualitative methods have recently felt the impact of computer applications.

Readers will be familiar with word processing applications and possibly data base and spreadsheet applications. All of these can help in qualitative work along with a small number of specialist applications that have been developed in recent years. Computers help qualitative researchers in a number of data treatment tasks that are repetitive or tedious, such as manipulating text in descriptive accounts, or finding and counting words (word processing), and keeping records of many instances, respondents, interviewees, etc. (data bases), or self-designed categorisation applications (spreadsheets).

Some specialist applications of computers include specialist categorisation tools, factor analysis tools for use with Repertory Grids (see p.111), Key Word in Context applications (see p.134) and other content and discourse analysis applications.

Apart from how *useful* the application of computers might be, there is also the question of how congruent the use of a mechanistic automated device is in qualitative research that is supposed to be human-being-based. Some would argue that incongruence arises because the use of computers even for mundane repetitive tasks removes the important human touch. It is argued that human beings sorting through data will see links and make fruitful mistakes that only people can make. Others see no problem in the use of computers to speed up an otherwise tediously lengthy mundane task.

Discourse Analysis

Although we have separated discourse analysis from the main body of content analysis, we see it as a specialist subdivision, dealing with language (as opposed to images; photos, film etc, music, symbols etc). The term *discourse analysis* is not used consistently in qualitative research literature. Some use it to refer to all research which focuses on language and linguistics, others use it in connection with studies looking at language differences and yet more people use the term to describe social psychology applications of a more general content analysis type.

All variations have language as the focus which for many puts it at the centre of human studies, owing to the uniqueness and central role of human language in the structure of human relationships. Another common feature of discourse analyses is the attention paid to the micro-components of language - individual words and phrases. These small units of discourse are analysed for meaning and then categorised and counted in the most structured examples.

Advantages: As for content analysis, but paying close attention to a uniquely human characteristic.
Disadvantages: As for content analysis, plus the concentration on small fragments can lose the contextual emphasis and therefore the meaning of the discourse.

Repetition of research cycle

As we have mentioned before, repeating the data treatment is in itself a data treatment technique. Repeating the research cycle (not just the data treatment) is also a valuable method of elaborating the data further. It serves a number of purposes:
- As a check on the trustworthiness of the data. If the results are the same the second time around, then the data is more likely to be stable and trustworthy.
- As a method of elaborating the data further. It would be very suspicious if the data was exactly the same upon repetition of the research cycle. Nothing in the human domain remains absolutely constant, so we might repeat the research cycle to

try to understand how things might have changed.
- To detect changes in the researcher(s). Since human beings are the measuring instruments as well, we can check on what might be affecting them over time by repeating the measurements.
- To check on first impressions. We may have had some 'gut reactions' the first time round, of which, if they persist through the repetition, we might take more notice.
- To review and refine tentative hypotheses. The process of developing or possibly testing hypotheses is a continuous one in qualitative work, so the researcher goes through the research cycle again in order to gather more information which may help confirm (or otherwise) initial hypotheses.

Advantages: Easy procedure to conduct, gives the findings a 'reliability and validity' check. Picks up changes in thoughts feelings attitudes in participants and researcher. Allows modification of procedure after collaboration.
Disadvantages: Time consuming, questionable benefit in terms of findings since it can be difficult to know how to interpret any differences between findings on different cycles.

Participant consultation

In keeping with the collaborative theme in qualitative work, a valuable data treatment method is to involve the participants, not only in data generation and collection, but also in the data treatment itself. This method is particularly appropriate for those researchers who wish their study to be involving, inclusive and non-alienating. Reason (1981) suggests that if researchers do not have, and carry out, an intention to involve the participants in the analysis, then they run the risk of being mere journalists.

Advantages: Pursues the participative or collaborative theme of qualitative study. Enhances the reliability and validity of findings.
Disadvantages: Few beyond time consuming nature of collaboration and associated people-management problems.

6 Presenting Qualitative Research

Reporting your work
At some point you may decide that you wish to report your work in some form, or it may be that you *have to*. If the latter is the case, then it is probable that the form your report must take will be determined by some other authority - the providers of the course or the organisation for whom the research has been conducted. Although there are conventions about the reporting of research there is, in qualitative research, considerable flexibility in the form that your report can take. This chapter will look mainly at the conventions, whilst giving some attention to the alternatives.

When planning your report, both its style and content, it is important to bear in mind the following:
- remember that the report is concerned with effective communication and this aim should be borne in mind when deciding on the form of the report,
- consider presenting your work in a form that is congruent with it, i.e. a formal report may not be 'right' for a self-analysis or autobiographical account of your therapy,
- consider the target audience for the report, particularly if the format has not been specified in advance
- reporting your work need not be a solo activity, and that advice, ideas and support may be gained from others,
- your research proposal will yield relevant material for the final report, and notes should be taken throughout your research, since relying on memory will produce a less accurate report.

Compare and Contrast # 8
(Reports)

The key word when it comes to presenting your findings is 'congruence'. Whether qualitative or quantitative, your report should be 'in the manner of' the research itself. To demonstrate this we will revisit the first **Compare and Contrast** and take some of the text from pages 14 and 15.

1. ...she visited the English department she asked the staff to help in her project. They agreed and got the students to write a story about arriving at college, based on what it was like for them. The staff then asked the students to write another story based on a perfect first week at an ideal college. Finally, the staff got the student group to make written recommendations to the college principal on how to improve the college 'welcome' to new students.

2. She wrote to all the other colleges in the region to find out how many had counselling services and of what type. She devised questionnaires for staff, students, parents and employers to find out whether a counselling service would be seen as an asset and whether students thought they would benefit from having someone to talk over their personal problems with. Finally, Aysha tabulated all her results and presented them in a written paper for the academic board.

3. He put a notice up in the staff common room asking if any other staff encountering the same problem would like to meet to discuss what they should do. Eight other tutors turned up to a meeting and decided to meet as a support group one lunchtime every week. Through talking about the problems that they suffered themselves as a consequence of listening to the problems of others, they got a clearer picture of what was needed in college to support students and the mostly untrained staff who listen. The group decided to invite some senior managers to one of their meetings to find out for themselves exactly what the problem was and how it affected students and staff.

Each method of reporting findings is congruent with the associated method of data collection. More 'conventionally' structured, formal reporting is generally associated with quantitative methods. Although qualitative research may have to be formal and adhere to certain conventions for publication, this is not always the case and it is worth holding out for your own preferred style. Below are further examples which illustrate the contrasting styles of formal quantitative report, participant's diary and autobiographical narrative:

'The split-plot ANOVA was carried out on the shift scores for each block of subjects x treatments. Shifts to caution were negatively scored, shifts to risk being positive.' Sanders (1974) p.16.

'I was troubled to discover my lack of honesty in filling in my data sheets. This took (at least) two identifiable forms:
    (a) I simply chickened out of putting sex down as often as I ought. I had no trouble with sexual activity or sexual interest/ attraction which was reciprocated. I did not log my private, covert sexual attractions, even towards SERG members with whom I had plenty of opportunities to check out the feelings.' Sanders (1986) p.14.

*'I have been thinking of this as 'the autobiographical chapter', but now, of course, I remind myself that **all** of this thesis is about my personal experience.....A problem about history - even individual history - is that there is so much of it. I have found myself recalling more and more incidents, images and texts, and have had to resist the possibility of this section taking over the whole thesis.'* Miller (1993) p.83.

The process of writing your report

• Allow time for the writing of the report - it is an integral piece of the research process rather than a tiresome addition to it. It is the means by which your research and findings will enter the public domain and offers the opportunity to make a positive contribution to the culture of which you are a part.

• When developing a timetable for your write-up, be aware of your preferences and working methods. It may be that you are advised to write a certain amount a day, but if you work better in bursts (binge writing) work this into your timetable. Similarly, if you work better at a certain time of day, recognise this fact.

• As this is written, the telephone is off the hook, other members of the household have been persuaded that elsewhere is a better place to be, and any callers will have to break the door down to gain entry. Attempt to recreate these conditions to the best of your ability - isolate yourself from distractions, and stick to the task of writing rather than tidying your desk, reading just one more article or cleaning the tiles in the bathroom!

• Do not get trapped in the 'masterpiece syndrome'. Your writing should be a clear, effective and congruent report of what you did, why you did it, and what you found, it does not have to be a work of art. To this end, choosing the appropriate format will be an advantage, since it helps discipline your style.

• Explain to others, or negotiate with others, why you need the time and how you will be using it, including any benefits to them.

Formal reports

Although there are opportunities for flexibility and creativity in the reporting of qualitative work, there may be occasions when a more formal or conventional report is required. Publication of research, whether qualitative or quantitative, brings its own set of restrictions. Glancing through research literature will give the impression that each publication has its own guidelines over format. Whilst this is true in the detail of the report, there are broad conventions which it is useful to bear in mind when preparing work for a formal report. Generally, the writer adopts a formal style of reporting and divides the report into a number of traditional or customary sections, the contents of which are fairly specific. This approach to report writing is covered in Sanders and Liptrot (1993) and the following is a precis of that description.

A 'journal style' report

Title page: The main topic of the report, plus name of author and institution and acknowledgements of support and funding.

Abstract: A brief and clear summary of the project, covering the aims, method and findings of the research. (Should be no more than 200 words)

Introduction: As its name suggests, this section introduces the work starting with a general introduction to the area, a definition of terms, theoretical or organisational context, a survey of relevant previous research and concluding by focusing on the present study - including hypotheses where appropriate.

Method: Technical details of the study, split into four subsections:
- Participants : number, characteristics, how selected (including exclusion criteria and procedures for non-participants).
- Materials: details of all materials used, with examples, explanations, coding procedures where necessary.
- Procedure: precise details of how the study was conducted (sufficient that the study could be replicated).
- Design: methodological issues and considerations.

Results: Clear and concise presentation of main points of analysed data (raw data should be included in an appendix).
Discussion: Analysis of results in relation to research questions or hypothesis. Relationship of findings to previous research or theory. Explanations of findings in terms of theory and problems identified by analysis of negative cases. Identification of issues raised and suggestions for further research.
References: Acknowledgement of all sources used in conducting research.
Appendices: All other materials not placed elsewhere in the report.

Approaches to reporting case studies
Case studies do not fit into the format described above, yet may need to be reported in a formal manner. When introducing the case study, there will be the need to explain the focus of the case study, for example with reference to the particular problem involved. Rather than a theoretical overview and reference to past studies, what will be necessary will be a description of the context within which the study occurred. It is also worth noting that this is an area where ethical problems may arise. It may be difficult to achieve a balance between the need to establish the context and nature of the problem or issue whilst maintaining the desired level of confidentiality or anonymity that was guaranteed to participants. Having established the context, this may be followed by description and analysis of the data or information derived from the study and evaluation of the process. Added to this information, but forming an addendum or appendix, details should still be provided of methodological considerations and procedures, adhering as closely as possible to the criteria described earlier for this section.

Having suggested that the case study technique is perhaps least suited to the journal approach, it is perhaps best suited to alternative formats of reporting, particularly *narrative* based approaches. This type of approach may also function most effectively in communicating the study to a non-academic readership. As suggested above, any technical details may be included in appendices, leaving a straightforward narrative account of the case as the basis for further consideration according to the needs of the reader.

Similarly, an *inverted structure* may have value in communicating findings and methodologies to the non-academic reader. Rather than building through technical detail to the findings of the study, the first section presents the findings and the rest of the report is devoted to explaining how the findings were arrived at.

Simple, but detailed *chronological reporting* (see p.128) of the case study can be highly effective for identifying cause and effect relationships. However, multiple case studies are unlikely to benefit from this sort of treatment as each would have to be reported separately and consecutively, thus effectively separating the elements which could otherwise have been compared.

A *question and answer* approach can provide a mixture of analysis and description. Questions may be posed and then answered with reference to any aspect of the case study. In particular, if multiple cases are being considered, application of the same questions to the different cases may be both interesting and illuminating for the reader. This is also true if the same case study is subjected to analysis within different theoretical frameworks, either by consecutive considerations using the different frameworks, or by adopting the question and answer approach, but answering each question a number of times each from a different perspective.

Other ways of presenting the information may include:
- diaries (particularly interesting if both client and counsellor accounts are included)
- video and audio tape recordings (remember permission and the difficulty of anonymity)
- photographic records,
- diagrams, drawings, cartoons.

Any of these may form the bulk of a report or be used to augment the main method chosen. Remember to discuss the appropriateness of inclusion with a supervisor.

Note: The above are simply suggestions rather than an exhaustive list of alternative approaches. If a particular structure has not yet been decided on, then further reading may be appropriate - you should of course have encountered different formats a the result of your literature search. Once again, this can be a valuable source of information beyond the data and findings of your study.

Reports required by others

If it is the case that the report you are preparing has been commissioned by an employer, or maybe is part of your job or a course assignment, then the format of the report will probably be specified. However, if there is a degree of flexibility, or a lack of guidelines, it is probably a good idea to stick to a slimmed down version of the journal approach. The term 'slimmed down' is apposite in this context - the people for whom it is being produced are unlikely to have either the time, or the inclination to digest the amount of information contained in a complete journal style report.

Having slimmed down the sections of the journal style report, it is then worth including appendices, so that readers with different interests will also be able to find the type of information they may require. Although other sections may be slimmed down, the one section that can be increased is the summary or abstract. A more detailed summary, running to a page or more, will allow for easy digestion of the main whats, whys, hows and findings of the research.

It may also be appropriate to accompany a technical report of this type with additional types of presentation - either oral, visual or a combination of the two. If an oral/visual presentation of the report is to be made, the following points may be useful, particularly if the presentation is to be made to potential funders:

• Do not present copies of the report at the same time as the oral presentation - make it available days prior to the presentation in order that the information can be pre-digested and questions prepared (anticipate these). Alternatively, have copies of the report available at the end of the presentation. There are few things more disheartening than people reading while you are trying to interest them in your presentation.

• Personally ensure that the necessary materials are present - do not assume that they will magically appear, or that they will simply be there. The present authors keenly remember assuming that a teaching room in a university would naturally contain all the required equipment, and were forced to construct their own flip-chart using pieces of blu-tack and pass around their lovingly prepared overhead projector films in the absence of either the required projector or a handy torch.

If the report is to include evaluation and recommendations, ensure that these are clearly related to the data obtained and reported in the study and are practical or achievable. Inevitably, there are possible ethical implications in the production of this type of report - to what extent may your reporting of your findings, your interpretation of the findings and your recommendations be subject to alteration or removal by the authority to which you must report? This question must be addressed before commencement of the research, as it may define the boundaries of the research, or allow you to make a decision as to whether the process is to be worthwhile, personally or professionally.

However, the above problem does not invalidate the process of presenting the findings to others prior to making your recommendations. The different perspectives they may offer may help in producing more appropriate recommendations. Remember that the findings are just that - information provided by the research tool. The findings may then be subjected to interpretation, viewed in the light of theoretical positions or judged according to particular values. So while the findings may remain unaltered, different researchers or individuals may interpret or judge the findings differently, according to their orientation or predisposition.

Communicating to a wider audience: use of the media
It may be that the findings of your research are deemed of sufficient interest and appropriateness to be of interest to a wider audience. Obviously, sending a copy of the final report (particularly in journal format) is unlikely to have a newspaper editor screaming, "Hold the

front page!" - in fact it's unlikely to be read by anyone in a busy office at all. For those who wish to communicate with the media, the requirements of a press or media release are fairly basic:

- *Masthead*: In practice your normal letter heading will suffice, this will allow the reader immediately to determine who the release is from.
- *Dateline*: When the release was issued, allowing the reader to determine whether it is current or not (and likely to still be current at publication time). You may wish to add an embargo (the date after which the information may be used).
- *Headline*: A short title explaining the subject of the release 'Counselling Saves Lives' may be preferable to 'Research has shown that people who use counselling services are less likely to attempt suicide'.
- *Text*: As a general rule, no more than one A4 sheet, typed and double spaced. If your story is of sufficient interest and requires more information, people will get back to you. As far as possible, start with What, Who, Where and Why and avoid jargon phrases and terms.
- *For further information*: Self explanatory, but vital, names, numbers and addresses of the best contacts for the person receiving the release.

Readers wishing more information on this subject are directed to *Hitting the Headlines: a practical guide to the media*, by White et al (1993), published by the British Psychological Society.

It probably hardly needs mentioning that opening up your research to a wider audience in this manner opens up yet another nest of ethical vipers. My favourite example is that of a friend who was scheduled to appear on a news magazine programme the day a general election was announced. He was contacted by the television company, who asked him to change the focus of the broadcast and sent a motorcycle courier to his house for a list of his proposed changes. He sent back a blank sheet of paper and watched the programme from his armchair, morally secure but having passed up his moment of fame.

References

Axline, V. (1964) *Dibs: In Search of Self.* Penguin Books (Published as Pelican in 1971).
Banyard, P. and Hayes, N. (1994) *Psychology: Theory and Application.* London: Chapman and Hall.
British Psychological Society (1978) *Ethical Principles for Research with Human Subjects.* Statement at AGM April 1978.
British Sociological Association (1989a) *BSA Guidelines on Anti-Sexist Language.* London: BSA.
British Sociological Association (1989b) *Anti-Racist Language: guidance for good practice.* London: BSA.
Butler, J.M. and Haigh, G.V. (1954) 'Changes in the relation between self-concept and ideal concepts consequent on client-centred counselling', **in** C.R. Rogers and R.F. Dymond (eds) *Psychotherapy and Personality Change.* University of Chicago Press.
Callaway, H. (1981) 'Women's perspectives: research as re-vision', **in** Reason, P. and Rowan, J. (eds) *Human Inquiry: A Sourcebook of New Paradigm Research.* Wiley.
Campbell, J.T., Daft, R.L. and Hullin, C.L. (1982) *What to Study: generating and developing research questions.* Newbury Park and London: Sage.
Collin, A. (1981) 'Mid-career change: reflections upon development of a piece of research and the part it has played in the development of the researcher.' **in** Reason, P. and Rowan, J. (eds) (1981) *Human Inquiry: A Sourcebook of New Paradigm Research.* Wiley.
Eichler, M. (1988) *Nonsexist Research Methods: a practical guide.* London: Unwin Hyman.
Festinger, L., Reicken, H.W. and Schachter, S. (1956) *When Prophecy Fails.* University of Minneapolis Press, Minneapolis.
Fransella, F. and Bannister, D. (1977) *A Manual for Repertory Grid Technique.* London: Academic Press.
Gergen, M. M. (1988) 'Building a Feminist Methodology.' *Contemporary Social Psychology,* **13**, 47-53.
Glaser, B.G. and Strauss, A.L. (1967) *The Discovery of Grounded Theory: Strategies for Qualitative Research.* Chicago: Aldine.
Glesne, C. and Peshkin, A. (1992) *Becoming Qualitative Researcher - an Introduction.* New York: Longman.

Handy, C.B. (1985) *Understanding Organisations (New Edition)*. Penguin.
Haney, C., Banks, W.C. and Zimbardo, P.G. (1970) 'Interpersonal dynamics in a simulated prison.' *International J. of Criminology and Penology*, **1**, 69-79.
Kagan, N. (1984) 'Interpersonal Process Recall: Basic Methods and Recent Research', in Larsen, D. *Teaching Psychological Skills*. Monterey California: Brooks Cole.
Kagan, N. and Krathwohl, D.R. (1967) *Studies in human interaction: Interpersonal Process Recall simulated by videotape*. East Lansing: Michigan State University.
Kelly, G. (1955) *The Theory of Personal Constructs*. New York: Norton.
Lewin, K. (1951) *Field Theory in Social Science: selected theoretical papers (edited by Cartwright, D.)*, New York: Harper and Row.
Liptrot, D. and Sanders, P. (1994) *An Incomplete Guide to Inferential Statistics for Counsellors*. Manchester: PCCS.
Lofland, J. and Lofland, L.H. (1984) *Analysing Social Settings: a guide to qualitative observation and analysis*. (2nd Edn). Wadsworth.
Maccoby, M. (1979), *The Gamesman*. Simon & Schuster.
Marsh, J. (1983) The Boredom of Study: A Study of Boredom. *Management Education and Development*, **14**, 120-135.
Maruyama, M. (1981) 'Endogenous research: the prison project.' in Reason, P. and Rowan, J. (eds) (1981) *Human Inquiry: A Sourcebook of New Paradigm Research*. Wiley.
Mead, M. *(1928) Coming of Age in Samoa*. Penguin.
Milgram, S. (1963) Behavioural study of obedience. *Journal of Abnormal Psychology*, **67**, 371-8.
Miller, N. (1993) *Personal Experience, Adult Learning and Social Research*. CRAEHD Publications, Thesis series.
Miller, N. and Brown, J. (1985) 'Researching the social economy of Conference 85', in *Group Relations*, Winter 1985.
Noblitt, G.W. and Hare, R.D. (1988) *Meta-Ethnography: synthesizing qualitative studies*. London: Sage.
Piliavin, I.M., Rodin, J. and Piliavin, J.A. (1969) Good Samaritanism: an underground phenomenon? *Journal of Personality and Social Psychology*, **13**, 289-99
Reason, P. 'An exploration in the dialectics of two-person relationships.' in Reason, P. and Rowan, J. (eds) (1981) *Human Inquiry: A Sourcebook of New Paradigm Research*. Wiley.
Reason, P. and Rowan, J. (eds) (1981) *Human Inquiry: A Sourcebook of New Paradigm Research*. Wiley.
Robinson, E.J. and Whitfield, M.J. (1987) Participation of patients during general practice consultations, *Psychology and Health*, **1**, 123-32.
Rogers, C.R. (1961) *On Becoming a Person: a therapist's view of psychotherapy*. London: Constable.

Sanders, P. (1974) *An investigation of shift on the risk dimension using simulated hypothetical discussion groups.* Unpublished thesis.
Sanders, P. (1986) 'A User's View of SERG', in *Group Relations,* Spring, 1986.
Sanders, P. and Liptrot, D. (1993) *An Incomplete Guide to Basic Research Methods and Data Collection for Counsellors.* Manchester: PCCS.
Spradley, J.P. (1980) *Participant Observation.* New York: Holt, Rinehart and Winston.
Stephenson, W. (1953) *The Study of Behaviour.* The University of Chicago Press.
Stephenson, W. (1980) 'Newton's Fifth Rule and Q-Methodology; applications to educational psychology. *American Psychologist,* **35**, 882-9.
White, S., Evans, P, Mihill, C. and Tyroe, M. (1993) *Hitting the Headlines - a practical guide to the media.* BPS Books.
Winter, D.A. (1967) 'Construct relationships, psychological disorder and therapeutic change. *British Journal of Medical Psychology,* **55** 257-69

Recommended further reading

The following are suggested for all those readers who wish to read some qualitative, new paradigm or action research related to counselling, therapy or interpersonal relationships. Whatever your interest, we would direct interested readers towards the referenced work. In particular, we have found the following enjoyable and inspirational:

Personal Experience, Adult Education and Social Research: developing a sociological imagination in and beyond the T-group, by Nod Miller (1993). Published by CRAEHD Publications and available from Centre for research in Adult Education for Human Development, University of South Australia. A$38.50.
(It may seem odd to recommend an expensive book from an Australian University, but we really found it uplifting.)

Human Inquiry: A Sourcebook of New Paradigm Research. Edited by Peter Reason and John Rowan (1981). Published by John Wiley & Sons.
(Widely available seminal book that is just about required reading.)

Doing Your Research Project - a guide for first time researchers in education and social sciences (2nd Edn), by Judith Bell (1993) Published by Open University Press.
(Practical guide to the production end of research once you know more-or-less what you're doing.)

Glossary

Accretion measure - the things that have been added to the environment or world by the action of humans.
Analysis - taking things or ideas apart, or separating things into their constituent parts to see how they fit together.
Analysis of negative cases - seeking an explanation of all of the instances that do not fit in with a hypothesis, theory or general trend in the results.
Attenuation - getting used to a stimulus, evidenced by a diminishing response strength.
Bias - any unwanted or undetected distortion that creeps into and colours the findings.
Calibration - setting the zero-point and checking the accuracy of an instrument against a known measure.
Case study - a way of investigating or exploring the world by following, describing and analysing a particular instance or case.
Coding - attaching values to events, observations or ideas. The plan or schedule that guides coding is called a *coding scheme*.
Comparative - any way of looking at the world that compares two or more things, e.g. comparing humans with other animals, comparing men with women, etc.
Construct - an idea that we create about how our world works and the 'things' that exist in it.
Contextualisation - putting something in a context.
Convenience and opportunity sample - a *sample* selected purely for convenience, when the opportunity arises.
Correlation - when two variables have a relationship though not necessarily a causal one.
Cross-sectional study - a study conducted at one point in time where participants or events are sampled from each of successive cohorts.

Demographic - statistics carrying information about human *populations*, e.g. age, sex, place of work, living conditions, etc.
Dualism - the idea that the mind and body are two separate entities.
Elaboration - extending, embellishing or further expanding on something in order to revel or discover meaning.
Empirical - relying on observation and measurement, not just theory or ideas.
Erosion measure - the degree of destruction, wear or negative action on the world or environment as a consequence of human living.
Evaluation studies - any study focusing on appraising, or estimating the value of something.
Experimental - following the *experimental method* in which all variables are *controlled* except one, which is manipulated by the experimenter.
Face validity (also surface validity) - where the validity of the measure is judged simply on whether it seems to be, or looks, appropriate.
Generalisation - the application of principles learned from a *sample* to the *population* from which the sample was drawn.
Grounded Theory - proposed by Glaser and Strauss (1967), a theory that is firmly and self-consciously rooted in the human experience of the theorists and phenomena that they try to explain and account for themselves.
Holism - taking the whole of something, e.g. a process or organism, rather than splitting into parts, also another term for *synthesis* (see below), e.g. applied to human illness as holistic medicine.
Hypothesis - a statement of belief about the world, that is, as yet, unknown.
Hypothetico-deductive method - a scientific method whereby we formulate a *hypothesis* that predicts what is going to happen in a given situation then test it.
Indigenous categories - categories developed or invented 'naturally' by groups of people in everyday life.
Inter-observer reliability - the degree to which two or more observers agree on what they've observed.
Longitudinal study - a type of study where subjects are tested at intervals over a period of time.

Methodology - the study or description of methods (e.g. in the social sciences).
Participant observation - variations on a general method where the observer is involved or participates in the action that is being observed. A dual-role.
Perceptual set - a habitual way of seeing things which predisposes us to see the world or events in it in a particular way.
Phenomenology - the philosophical belief that our knowledge is based on our experience, on attending to phenomena as they are directly and subjectively experienced.
Population - the total number of people, objects, events or measurements sharing one or more features.
Positivism - a philosophical idea that there is a fixed observable world which we all experience in a similar way. Knowledge is limited to observed facts and that which can be deduced from those facts.
Primacy and recency effect - an effect due to the fact that people remember the first and last things in a list better than the middle things.
Qualitative - a non-numerical method which appreciates the characteristics or features of a person or event rather than a measurement of the size of those characteristics.
Quantitative - a numerical measurement of characteristics of people or events.
Random sample - this is a *sample* selected by chance.
Raw data - data that is in its 'just collected' form and therefore unrefined and in need of organisation.
Reductionism - *analysis* where an explanation is reduced to its simplest constituents.
Reliability - also called *consistency*. It refers to the likelihood of getting the same results repeatedly if the measure is conducted in the same circumstances.
Representative sample - this is a sample that contains within it all of the essential characteristics of the *population* from which it is drawn in the correct proportions.
Sample - any part of a *population* specified by the person taking the sample.
Sampling - the act of taking or selecting a sample.

Selective attention - paying attention to only part of the world at any given time. Humans are naturally selective in what they pay attention to.

Simulation - specially organised event where some of the features of real-life are replicated in order to simulate the real world. Observations or measurements are then made.

Survey - any study trying to measure, explore, review or map out opinions, attitudes or other human qualities by looking at many people.

Synthesis - putting things together in familiar or novel ways to see what patterns are made and to understand how they might fit and work together.

Test-retest reliability -taking of repeated measurements and *correlating* them.

Triangulation - finding the location of something by taking measurements from two or more different positions. In qualitative studies; using more than one method of collecting and interpreting data to elaborate or understand the same phenomenon.

Validity - when a measure measures what it claims or intends to measure.

Variable - anything that can vary, change and be measured.

Index

Main entries only

Action, 65
    research, 115
Axline, V., 28
Banyard, P., 24, 86, 87
Behavioural counselling, 10
Behaviourism, 10
British Assoc. for Counselling, 57
British Psychological Society, 23, 148
British Sociological Assoc., 23
Butler, J.M., 106
Calibration, 35
Case studies, 28
    how to organise, 29
Chronologies, 128
Coding, 122
    pre-determined, 84
Collaboration, 65
Collin, A., 74
Computers, 134
Content analysis, 130
    categorisation, 132
    context issues in, 132
    sampling in, 131
    units of record in, 131
Contexts and motives, 17
Control, and structure, 107
Cover stories, 38
Data,
    categorising, 124
    coding, 122
    collection, 63
    computers in, 134
    describing, 125
    methods of collection, 122
    raw, 6
    sorting, 127
    treatment of, 5, 117
    what is it, 64, 117

Davies, G., 60
Diaries, 97
Discourse analysis, 136
Documents and records, 109
Eichler, M., 21
Ethics, and counselling, 57
    and research, 58
Evaluation studies, 31
Feminist research, 20
Festinger, L., 71
Fransella, F., 106, 111
Gaining access, 40
Gergen, M., 23
Glaser, B.G., 121
Glesne, C., 39
Handy, C.B., 128
Haney, C., 76
Human inquiry groups, 76
Humanism, 10
Interpersonal Process Recall, 106, 113
Interviews, 98
    fully structured, 102
    planning, 99
    semi-structured, 102
    setting, 101
    structure of, 100
    unstructured, 104
Journals and logs, 74
Kagan, N., 106, 113
Kelly, G., 111
Key Word in Context, 134, 135
Language, 136
Letters, 98
Lewin, K., 65, 115
Location, 41
    of an interview, 101
Lofland, J., 83
Maccoby, M., 128

Marsh, J., 106, 114
Maruyama, M., 71
Mead, M., 70
Media, use of, 147
Meta analysis, 114
Memo writing, 73
Milgram, S., 75
Miller, N., 75, 76, 77, 109, 116, 141
Negative cases, 48
Noblitt, G.W., 114
Observer bias, 86
    as participant, 70
    effects, 78
    installation as, 77
Observation,
    non-participant, 69
    participant, 68
    recording of, 77, 81
    self, 72
Participants, choosing, 43
    consulting with, 137
    and data, 65
    observation, 68
Person-centred approach, 10
Physical traces, 109
Piliavin, I.M., 75
Pilot study, 48, 133
Presentation of research, 139
    case studies, 144
    formal reports, 143
    journal style, 143
    media, 147
    question and answer, 145
Proposal, 50
Published media, 109
Q-Methodology, 106, 115
Qualitative methods,
  definition of, 1-3, 17
Quantitative methods,
  definition of, 1-3, 17
Questions, closed, 89
    open, 90
    principles of asking, 91

Questionnaire, 93
    semi-structured, 95
    setting, 93
Racist language, 23
Rapport, 43
Reason, P., 1, 74, 76, 137
Reliability, 46
Repertory Grid approach, 106, 111
    and computers, 135
    technique, 111
Repetition, 66
    of research cycle, 136
Research,
    location of, 41
    proposal, 50
Researcher, role of, 3
Robinson, E.J., 69
Rogers, C.R., 115
Role play, 74
Rowan, J., 1, 74, 76
Sampling, 81
Sanders, P., 77, 141
Sexist language, 23
Simulation, 74
Spradley, J.P., 82
Stephenson, W., 106, 115
Structure, and control, 107
Supervision,
    and counselling, 58
    and research, 58
Time, chronologies, 128
    management, 56
Triangulation, 47
Trustworthiness, 44
Typologies, 127
Validity, 46
Variables and measurement, 4
White, S., 148
Winter, D.A., 112
Womens' perspectives, 20
Zimbardo, P.G., 76